CW01496079

For
Lucy, Amy, Chloe and Harriet

How Your Practice Can Beat The Recession

(The Dental Marketing Secrets You Need To Succeed)

By

Neil Sanderson

Published by Sanderson Media
Bedfordshire, England

DENTAL
MARKETING EXPERT

About the Author

NEIL SANDERSON Has been involved with sales and marketing for some of the largest global IT companies since 1982 achieving "top sales" awards at each of them, these companies included Xerox and Digital Equipment Company.

In addition to the success he has enjoyed with the above companies his entrepreneurial spirit has led him to create a number of companies before his latest venture, "Dental Marketing Expert Ltd."

He has been involved with the dental profession since 1993 when he launched his first dental practice management software company. From the very start the company has seen year on year growth. During that whole period Neil has been responsible for the business development of the company which today has annual revenues of $20m.

His latest venture "Dental Marketing Expert" is dedicated to improving the revenues, profits and customer loyalty of its clients by the implementation of his unique knowledge of specialist dental marketing techniques.

Table of Contents

How Your Practice Can Beat The Recession
(The dental marketing secrets you need to succeed)

Chapter One
Surviving in a 21st century recession

"Average pay for dentists fell in the 2009/10
The average taxable income for dentists in England and Wales fell
from £89,600 in the 2008/09 year to £84,900 in 2009/10.

In the Dental Earnings and Expenses, England and Wales, 2009/10
report the 5.2% decrease relates to dentists who have carried out
some NHS work, but takes both public and private income into
consideration.

Expenses were also looked at in the report, which were found to have
risen by 3.1% for the average practice with the rising cost of
equipment, dental ware, staffing and regulation/red tape blamed for
the increase"

Here was another headline on the 7/10/2011

"Chair of BDA says now is the worst time to be a dentist
Dr Susie Sanderson (no relation) has announced that she believes
now is the worst time in living memory to be a dentist in the UK, in a
blog on the British Dental Association (BDA) website.

The chair of the BDA's executive board said, "the factors which have
combined to give her this opinion include too much regulation,

uncertainty about NHS pensions and flaws in the 2006 dental contract".

She said "That isn't a statement I make lightly or happily but sadly it is one I make fairly and confidently".

Looking toward the future she expressed hope that moves such as pilots, which were launched last month, will lead to better contracts and the transfer of commissioning responsibilities to the National Commissioning Board will mean more consistency".

These were two of the headlines in October 2011, not good news and it might just get worse.

As I write this book the UK economy is technically not in recession, the economy is bumping along the bottom of a very uncomfortable trough, which we appear to be well and truly anchored into.

Growth in the economy is around 0.1% and if we read the news is likely to get a whole lot worse.

Whilst we may not officially be in a recession I think that you would all agree that it certainly feels like one, there appears to be gloom, doom and despondency everywhere you look and the news just seems to go from bad to worse.

The Euro Zone is pretty much bankrupt along with the United States and just about every economist is telling us that a double dip recession or even another great depression may be on the cards.

Whether or not we actually go into official recession or not is anybody's guess and I am no expert in this field so we'll just have to trust the bankers and politicians to keep us on the right side of the line.

I have seen recessions in the 1970's, 80's, 90's and now this one, which kicked off with the crash of the banking industry in 2008. The main difference between this one and all the others were that people's overall spending habits didn't change that much and the recessions were relatively short lived.

This one is different; I have observed a marked change in the way people now view the economy, their spending habits and their general outlook on life.

From the days of Margaret Thatcher to 2008 most young people expected at some point to be able to get onto the housing ladder and buy their own home, that is not now the case, in fact the opposite is now the norm as most people are struggling to pay high rents and can't afford a 20 or 25% deposit on their mortgage.

Equally many, if not all, business people expected the banks to help them out to start a business or grow their business, again this has now changed and most people expect to be turned down by requests for help from the bank.

I don't really know how to describe it but there is a very different feel in 2011 to all the other economic downturns and the general consensus is that this is going to be around for a very long time to come.

You may or may not agree with my views on this, if I'm wrong, things will bounce back next year and the banks will start lending again and the housing market will once again become buoyant, then you can forget what I'm going to say in this book, if on the other hand you think there may be something to what I have to say keep reading.

Most companies large and small are quite rightly trying to save money and pull in their horns, every penny has to be justified, every project scrutinised and then approved and they're all cutting their marketing budgets.

Large corporations start each financial year with a new marketing budget and I can't really argue with that point (except that if you find that something is really working well why would you cap it?).

It also has to be said that over the last three of four years every large company has cut its marketing budget, this is a huge mistake. Just think about it, the economy is bad, sales are down and profits are down so lets cut our marketing spend. Guess what happens next? You've got it, sales go down, profits go down, the economy shrinks etc. etc. etc.

Now I'm not advocating that every company slashes every budget except the marketing budget as I fully understand why they do it and that's because just about every company has absolutely no idea whether their marketing is working or not.

They produce lovely glossy newspaper and magazine adverts, they produce great TV and radio ads and we watch them and say isn't that clever or amazing or funny, the problem is that the company that commissioned the advert usually has absolutely no idea whether or not the advert has worked or worse still what was its purpose.

I have worked for many large companies and seen at first hand how this works (or doesn't as is normally the case). The company will employ some very expensive advertising agency or a web development company who will come up with some sort of branding plan, which is designed to "improve the recognition of the brand".

Or better still they'll come up with a series of glossy adverts, all of which look stunning but nobody has actually tested.

They even change the name of the company or product without any concerns as to what this may actually do to sales so long as it "builds the brand".

These companies pay millions of pounds to have web sites that look the part, keep strictly to the rules of branding but which nobody visits and those individuals that do visit them seldom buy anything as a result.

It may be OK to waste all this money when you are a multi-million pound company but unfortunately I'm not and I suspect neither are you. You need customers, not a brand.

So I'm not here to tell you how to get your brand out there or tell you how to produce glossy adverts, videos, web sites, I'm going to share with you how to survive this recession (official or not) and not only survive it, I will show you how you can grow your business too.

You have to adapt your business to this new world we live in, or you will see your income and the income of your partners, staff, family etc. shrink, or worse still you'll go out of business its as stark as that.

Most dental practices and the companies that supply dental practices are not using marketing as the key to survival.

They are in fact sat hoping something will change, the economy will pick up, or there will be a second coming or something, well what are you going to do if it doesn't pick up and nothing changes except for the worse?

There is only one way to grow your business and that is through marketing, even brilliant sales people can't sell if they have no leads. The accounts department will only tell you how your company is doing financially. Your IT department (if you have one) will only get in the way and tell you what isn't possible and worst of all if you employ an HR department, well enough said about that one.

Just think about all the most successful companies over the years, they have all got where they are, not by having the best products or services but how they marketed them even the great Apple Corporation.

The big change in Apple's fortunes was the iPod, which lets face it when it first came out was just another MP3 player, but instead of telling us how many Megabytes it had, Apple told us how many songs it could store and guess what, they had the songs you wanted to buy on this web site called iTunes, do you see what I mean?

Now I am one of Apples biggest fans and they have some incredible products, in fact I'm writing this book now on one, a Mac, but its not just brilliant products that got Apple to where they are, its mainly brilliant marketing.

I have never had the pleasure of meeting Richard Branson but he is someone who I truly admire, he started his empire from virtually nothing and is now a multi billionaire.

And why do you think he has managed to reach these dizzy heights, well I can tell you it isn't because he has the best accounting department in the world or the best web designers or even the best Human Resources department.

No it's because he has tirelessly devoted himself to self promotion. I've absolutely no doubt he desperately wanted to fly across oceans in a balloon or take on British Airways in the courts, but all the time he managed to get it onto the 9.00 o'clock news or the front page of the newspapers.

I've flown Virgin Airlines on many occasions and without doubt they are a very nice airline, however are they the best, the biggest? Probably not, but they are without doubt one of the most recognisable, maybe even more so now than British Airways.

Sorry about the little diversion but you need to understand that the only way you can grow your practice/business through this recession is by clever, targeted quantifiable marketing and if anyone has a better solution I don't know about it.

So you may be the best dentist in town or have the best product to supply the dental profession with, but if nobody knows about you or your amazing product or service, how do you expect to make any money from it.

So unlike other coaches, consultants or experts I'm not going to tell you how to deal with your staff, or what colour to paint your surgery, what uniforms your nurse should wear or even how much you should be charging, all that is important when you've actually got a patient or customer through the door, but if that hasn't happened you need to read on.

Chapter Two
Food for Thought

The subject of marketing in the dental profession is almost a dirty word in some circles, the amount of times I've heard the words "I don't have to sell" are quite astonishing. It's quite true that for some time all a dentist had to do was open a practice in a high street and put up an "open for business sign" and hey presto the place was overflowing with patients.

And up until fairly recently there has been a general lack of dental practices for patients to attend. I still hear amongst my friends and colleagues the phrase "you simply can't get to see an NHS dentist". I think they haven't looked recently because as you are probably aware that situation has now changed quite radically.

I've heard many dental professionals tell me that "they do no marketing at all". OK, so how do their customers/patients know they exist? Is it some celestial body urging them to attend the practice, or might it actually be people talking about them?

In the UK during the course of the 1990's and Noughties there was a head long rush out of the National Health Service (NHS) and into private practice for all sorts of reasons which I'm not going to go into in this book, most practitioners did this very successfully and without really having to try to sell the concept to their patients. It was almost a case of this is how I now do business (yes sorry I have to use that term) and if you want to continue using this practice you will have to become a private patient or join Denplan (the largest dental insurance company in the UK) or one of the other insurance providers.

I can remember my own dentist who, after sending me a letter explaining that the next time I saw him would be the last on the NHS, but after that I would need to become a private patient.

When I arrived at the practice I noticed that nothing at all had changed except for the fact that all the staff were now proudly wearing Denplan badges.

I duly had my usual examination and scale and polish (which is all I'd actually had other than one filling for the last ten years) and I think I paid £18.00.

Once the treatment had finished he advised me that I now had a Denplan score and that I should go and see the Denplan representative. Being the somewhat awkward person that I am, I asked him what new and improved facilities was he going to put in place and would he be using better materials etc.

He informed me that the main benefit was that he wouldn't have to deal with the NHS any longer. So I asked again what would the new arrangement do for me, to which he looked totally bemused and again explained that he now didn't have to do all that form filling and he would be free of the NHS red tape. At which point I gave up and went to see the Denplan representative.

I'm not quite sure what my dental score was but she gleefully informed me that I fitted into band C and as a result my monthly fee would be £15.00. Now remember this was the 1990's and an examination, scale and polish on the NHS was around £18.00 each time, so I quickly did my sums and worked out that to get exactly the same treatment as I had been receiving for the last ten years would now be costing me £180.00 per year, as opposed to the £36.00 per year I was currently paying.

I have absolutely no problem with premium pricing, at the end of they day none of us buy on price, but you have to be able to sell and/ or justify your pricing, you can't simply tell your customers I'm increasing my prices by 3-400% without some sort of justification.

I apologise if you think that I am anti private dentistry, as this is definitely not the case, but the point was that my dentist, who I had known for the last ten years and I trusted implicitly, lost a valuable customer (patient), simply because he didn't sell the concept to me.

If he or his staff had tried to do a little marketing/sales to me I might have stayed with him. But he didn't, sorry Andrew if you're reading this now, no hard feelings.

I subsequently changed to another dentist (who incidentally was completely private) but he did take the time to explain to me what he did, how he cared for his patients etc. and I was more than happy to part with my hard earned cash.

So how did I find this new dentist, well back then towards the end of the 1990's I did what just about every single other person did, I opened the Yellow Pages, went to the dentist section and effectively stuck a pin in one of the adverts that caught my eye and hey presto he had a new customer (patient).

I would hope that that story doesn't sound familiar to you and I'm sure that you would never be quite as naive as my dentist was. I have no idea how he's now doing incidentally, hopefully very well.

I know that many dentists are very good at marketing themselves and their practices, there are some excellent business people out there and I have seen some very impressive web sites that have been produced probably at great cost.

I have even heard some dental practices advertise on the local radio, so don't get me wrong I know that there are many very able business individuals out there making a great deal of money and I take my hat off to them all.

Chapter Three
My Background

I have to confess that I was one of the worst pupils I know, basically I did not like school and all I could really think of was how quickly I could get out of it and do something else.

Back in the 1970's, being a working class lad in rural East Yorkshire, going to University was never really a consideration. I'm sure some of my peers did go on to further education, but I can't remember any of my class mates talking about going to "Uni". Everyone just discussed football, the latest pop records, girls and what job they would be going into when they left school.

Being the young entrepreneur I had my first paper round when I was ten years old which probably wouldn't even be legal nowadays, in fact the paper bag I was given almost came down to my ankles. I can remember hating Friday night paper rounds as they had the thickest papers, and loving Saturday as there was barely anything in them and we got paid on Saturday (eight shillings and six pence old money) - a fortune as I remember.

After a couple of years of doing the paper round I heard that there was a part time job going at the local printing works which I duly applied for and got aged 13, this brought me into the big bad world of commerce and yes I was sent to the local store for a "Long Stand" and "Sky Hooks", which everyone except me thought was hilarious.

So when I reached the heady age of fifteen I was given the choice by the then boss of the printing works, who told me in his best Yorkshire accent "you can have an apprenticeship now lad but if you stay on at school and do your 'O' level exams there won't be a job for you". So I made my first real business decision and decided to leave school and take up the offer of a printing apprenticeship. I have to say I have never regretted the decision.

A year or so later into my new career as a "Printing Journeyman" my mother informed the family that she was moving to York with her new boyfriend (soon to be husband) and I could either move with her or stay where I was. So I decided to move to the bright lights of York, where I got a job at the Yorkshire Evening Press and carried on my career in printing.

I can always remember finally gaining my City and Guilds certificate at the end of my apprenticeship, which meant that I was now a fully qualified compositor in the printing trade. Unfortunately this was just the time when new technology was coming into the trade and most, if not all, the skills I'd learnt over the past five years were now pretty much irrelevant. I still have my old "setting stick" which is what we used to produce words and sentences using lead letters, it now might even be worth something as an antique and a relic from the past, such is life!

Anyway after several jobs in the printing trade, which culminated in me being the top sales person for "Linotype" a company who sold electronic typesetting machines which were incredibly expensive, but the commission paid was very good.

At the tender age of 26, I started my first business, in which I started with one of my sales colleagues selling photocopiers in Liverpool.

We had absolutely no experience of photocopiers whatsoever, other that the fact I had made copies of my expenses etc over the years.

This was a real stab in the dark and all I had to move the business forward was a huge amount of enthusiasm, determination and pig headedness.

Somehow we managed to talk the local bank manager into loaning us £30,000 with the help of the government, in the form of a regional loan guarantee arrangement. We duly signed the lease on some large premises in the centre of Liverpool. We ripped the place apart and put in new carpets, furniture etc and had the swankiest photocopier show room in the city, we were very proud of ourselves and ready to take on the world.

We had a grand opening ceremony in which all our friends and family were invited along with a very small number of prospective customers, as we didn't have any actual ones at the time.

Things went very well at first, in fact so well that we won the accolade of being the top performing Canon copier dealer in the North West 1983/4. This was really quite amazing based on the fact that many of the other dealers had been doing this for some years and Liverpool in the 1980's with Derek Hatton and the "Crazy Gang" in the town hall, was not the easiest places in the world to build a business.

There was a very funny episode during that first year. Canon announced a new fax machine. Now remember at that time in the early 1980's nobody had fax machines. If you wanted to send written communications around the world you had a telex machine.

So we duly invited as many of our customers as we could to a demonstration of this great new technology. The the only way we could show how it worked was by having one fax machine in one office and another 30 feet down the corridor in another. People were amazed that you could send a document from one machine to another.

However we sold very few because the biggest objection was that nobody else had a fax machine to send your documents to, I suppose Alexander Graham Bell had the same problem when he invented the telephone.

As a reward for all this effort and sales and marketing genius, Canon rewarded us by appointing three more dealers in the Liverpool area as well as setting up a direct sales team. This meant that the majority of our competitors were now selling exactly the same brand of photocopier as we were.

Now I'm not going to complain about my lot, but we initially went to Canon gaining the exclusive Liverpool dealership, with a pretty good business plan, lots of enthusiasm and loyalty to the brand etc. Our plan was built on achieving around a 40% margin on the photocopiers we sold. Canon bought into this wholeheartedly.

As a result of Canon's decision to change our terms, we no longer had an exclusive area at all and our margins inevitably suffered. There are only two ways you can make a sale against someone else who is selling exactly the same piece of equipment as you are, and that is either to sell yours cheaper or sell the benefits of buying from you, rather than another dealer or Canon direct.

Selling against Canon direct was pretty difficult as they could always undercut us and it was also difficult to say that your service would be better than the people who actually manufactured the equipment.

Inevitably the day came in 1986 when the business went into receivership and I lost my house, car and pretty much everything else and just to add insult to injury, my business partner disappeared off the face of the earth never to be seen again leaving me with a mountain of debt.

I always thought that banks and finance houses would chase people who defaulted on their financial commitments. Sadly this is not the case and if there is an easy target e.g. the person who is left behind with family etc. that is the person they will target and I saw their bullseye.

I am quite proud to say that even with this set back and what were frightening debts, I did not go bankrupt and managed to pay off all my creditors over the next five years or so. I still don't know if this was the best course of action but that's what happened. I eventually even lost my desire to do unspeakable things to my ex-partner who as far as I am aware is living the life of luxury somewhere at my expense, not that I'm bitter or anything (thanks for everything Neville).

So I went back into the selling business and once again seemed to excel at this as I did reasonably well, made myself a few quid and climbed the corporate ladder.

By 1999 I was managing some of the largest corporate accounts in the UK for "Digital Equipment Company" (this used to be the worlds second largest computer company after IBM). Back in those days the most expensive computer in my price book cost in excess of two million pounds, and can you believe a 2Gb disk drive cost £18,000 and what's more, companies bought them by the bucket load.

We used to be able to go into the likes of British Gas, ICI, Procter and Gamble even Central Government etc. and ask how much they would be spending with us and then explain what they could have (things were different then). In 1991 I sold in excess of £10m of computer hardware, earning myself the heady accolade of being one of the top ten sales people in the world for DEC, which meant an all expenses paid trip to Boston USA, yippee.

Whilst I was basking in all this glory an ex-colleague of mine from Xerox called me and asked if I would like to meet him with a view to start a business with him. He had partnered with a US company (Viking Software) to sell "Data Entry" software and would like me to joint them.

After some negotiation and rather a lot of Yorkshire beer, I agreed to leave my cosy job at Digital Equipment and join him in this brand new adventure selling "Data Entry Software".

Now you might be scratching your head wondering what "Data Entry Software" is, because I certainly was, I had absolutely no idea what it did, who used it, how we could market it etc. but being the born entrepreneur (or idiot) I was, I went enthusiastically into this venture.

One slight draw back we had when we started this business was that whilst we sold "Data Entry Software" we didn't actually own a computer, although we did have a typewriter and a telephone.

So we started writing to and phoning lots of companies who we guessed would be using 'Data Entry". As it turned out data entry was pretty much a dying animal and most companies didn't want lots of ladies sat in front of computers, entering thousands of paper forms, which would then be fed into large computers (like the one's I had sold them). What they actually wanted was to have "on-line" applications that meant you could do away with the large central computer and scale down to a "client – server model", as you can imagine this was a bit of a problem for us guys selling data-entry.

We eventually managed to sell one or two systems, which meant that we could now buy a computer to demonstrate our product I really do wonder how we sold those early software systems without. I can only think that our first customers must have had incredible faith in me.

When we actually had a computer to demonstrate on, things became a little easier, although most companies still didn't really want data entry, they wanted online systems. After a great deal of work and making enquiries, we landed several lucrative contracts particularly with American Express (credit card slips) and Thomas Cook (travellers cheques), we were now very much on our way and even had a couple of staff on the payroll too, although there was many a month when we could not afford to pay ourselves.

It was around this time that my partner in the company began to spend most of his time in the local public houses, than in the office and yours truly took on the lion's share of generating new customers and making the place work. It became a joke between the staff, that if Mike wasn't in the pub he could usually be found on the golf course (I've never been very good at picking business partners).

Around this time in late 1992 I went down to Eastbourne to visit the then Dental Practice Board with a view to sell them a brand new Data Entry System, to replace their ageing system.

Now for those of you who are not based in England or Wales the "Dental Practice Board" were the body which paid dentists for

National Health Service (NHS) work. At this time millions of dental claim forms were processed by this organisation.

During my visit and subsequent tour of the establishment, I was informed that what they really wanted, was for the dental practices to input the forms back in their practices, so they wouldn't have to enter all these claim forms, which believe you me, there were millions of them piled as high as you can imagine.

They even said that they were giving every dental practice that sent their claims by electronic means a grant of £900 towards the cost of the equipment. A cunning plan began to hatch in my head.

This "Data Entry Software" that I had now become fairly familiar with was designed to mimic the paper forms that the data entry operators had to bash in by the thousand. And maybe we could make our software look like the good old FP17 form (the form used to make an NHS claim).

I duly went back to our software experts and put the idea to them. Initially they were very sceptical but after a while they came around to the idea and we decided to develop something.

I'm not going to go into the details but basically we wrapped the application in a simple database, put some data transmission software at the back end of it and produced a very simple application that would store patients details, allow you to search on them and enter an FP17 claim and transmit to the DPB.

I then went to a computer distributor and did a deal, whereby we could buy a computer, modem and printer for around £550, this meant we could sell the complete system for £900 and make a profit.

Finally in 1993 we were ready with a product, but we were still called "Viking Software", which doesn't really resonate with the Dental profession so we created a new company and called it "Dentrak".

This was about the time I discovered that I was reasonably good at marketing. I designed a three way-folding brochure which said very little about the software but explained how EDI (Electronic Data Interchange) worked and how simple it was to transmit your forms to the DPB, rather than put a paper form in the post. Best of all, dentists could effectively have a computer system for free (after the £900 grant). On every page there was a big "Call this number now for your free system"

To say this was a success was an understatement, in the first three months we sold fifty systems; we were so busy we literally couldn't keep up with demand, we didn't have enough trainers, engineers or even sales people to take the orders.

Now I am the first to admit Dentrak was never the best dental software product on the market, but that's not the point. It was exactly the right product at the right time. Time after time we see what is often inferior products champion much better ones because they get their marketing right, and we did just that.

Let me tell you a story of when I became the biggest hate figure amongst my dental software competitors and particularly the Dental Software Suppliers Association or DSSA.

Now for those of you who have never heard of the DSSA they were the body that represented the interests of some of the companies that supplied dental software systems to the UK market and they did not like Dentrak, we were a set of upstarts who had no right to produce a system for this price.

Not being one to court popularity I didn't really care that the DSSA did not want us to join their organisation, even though we did apply. They wouldn't even give us a reason why we could not join, maybe we weren't selling dental systems to the right sort of dentists?

So on with the story, before any company can sell a software product which can transmit claims to the Dental Practice Board you had to become accredited by them, this meant your software had to pass lots of data tests and effectively prove that your software works.

We did all the tests and duly became accredited. When you gained accreditation, the DPB sent you a very nice certificate and the right to carry the DPB logo on your literature to show that you had their accreditation.

The DPB at that time sent out all its correspondence on cream coloured paper and used cream coloured envelopes with their logo on the front. So I came up with the following plan.

We would print a letter on a single sheet of cream A4 without our own logo on it and insert it into a cream envelope, again without our own logo on it, just the DPB accreditation logo.

At no time did we claim to be representing the DPB or claim to be an agent of the DPB, we simply said that the Dentrak system was available for £900, there was a grant for £900, and that you should call this number to place your order.

The phones once again ignited into a frenzy of activity firstly from dentists placing orders for the £900 system and secondly form the DSSA complaining about our alleged underhand tactics.

This controversy continued to brew and eventually the DPB became involved. They agreed that we had broken no rules and had made no claims that were not completely true, however they did ask us not to do any more marketing of this type we duly complied to their request.

We were never allowed to join the DSSA even though we made several applications over the years. I am firmly of the belief that I came up with the idea of sending out the mailer that all of them wished they had thought of. We sold over a hundred systems as a result of that one mailer, bringing in over a hundred and fifty thousand pounds of revenue; I was and still am of the persuasion that he who dares wins.

The first versions of Dentrak worked on the MS DOS (Microsoft Disk Operating System) platform (for those of you who don't remember DOS it's the operating system that most computers worked on before the advent of Microsoft Windows). It was a very simple system but our customers loved it.

In 1997 we acquired another practice management software product from one of our competitors (AMCO) who had a system that utilised Microsoft Windows and could be networked. It also had a clinical charting module etc. We continued to sell the good old DOS system, due to demand but the new system quickly became the norm. We called this Dentrak Plus.

Our biggest two competitors at that time were Software of Excellence and Arthur; I have to admit that both these systems were far superior to Dentrak Plus.

We had only one developer where they had many, they also had more sales staff, but with what I believe was excellent marketing and very good sales skills, we managed to run them neck and neck for monthly sales.

By 2001 relations between my business partner and myself were not perfect. He was spending less and less time in the office, to the extent that some weeks we wouldn't see him at all. When he did actually make an appearance, he usually ended up upsetting members of staff or me, or both and quite frankly I was becoming fed up with the situation.

It was around now that this new American owned company called PracticeWorks were starting to make an impression on the dental software market place.

PracticeWorks was owned by two very wealthy entrepreneurs, they had already acquired several US dental software companies, which had given them a very large market share in the States. Because of regulatory rules they could not make any more acquisitions, so they were now looking for companies to buy in the UK.

Their first acquisition was a dental software company called Trident, quickly followed by SDS; between these two companies they now had a customer base of around 600 dental practices, (a similar size to Dentrak).

We were now fighting three very large competitors in Software of Excellence, Arthur and the new PracticeWorks, and as things between my partner and myself were not brilliant, when the latter came knocking on our door to see if we would be prepared to sell, I immediately warmed to the idea.

So in 2002 we sold Dentrak to PracticeWorks and as part of the agreement I headed up Sales and Marketing for the new company, which now had around 1200 practices using its software.

At the end of 2002 we acquired Arthur and Trophy Imaging, which meant we now had our own digital x-ray company and we were the single largest supplier of practice management software in both the US and now the UK.

In 2002 the company was turning over around $3m per annum and it was my job as head of sales and marketing to increase that substantially year on year.

In 2003 the company was sold by the two American individuals to Kodak for $500m, this made two people who were already very rich a lot richer still. I have to say that Richard and Jim are two of the nicest people I have ever met; you would have never known that they were multi millionaires.

As a result of the acquisition of the company by Kodak, PracticeWorks became part of the Kodak Health Group. I had to manage the campaign to rebrand it to Kodak Dental Systems, which sounds as difficult as it was.

We were already struggling to get the PracticeWorks name out into the market, remember most of our customers had bought Arthur, Dentrak, SDS or Trident systems so confusion reigned supreme.

However with a lot of advertising, direct mail and telesales activity we got the new brand out there. Having Kodak in the name didn't do us any harm it has to be said. Kodak at the time had a very strong brand, in fact one of the most recognisable brands in the world.

It was during this time that I came up with the concept of the "Integrated Digital Practice".

Kodak Dental Systems, as they were known then, were the only company who designed, manufactured and supported Dental Practice Management Software and all the digital imaging products that surround it. All our other competitors could offer part of the solution but not the whole thing and it was this that I concentrated on.

I designed the circle of products and the following advert appeared in the press. This was so successful that one of the largest dealers in the UK approached us with a view to exclusively selling the whole range of our products, including software (we didn't take them up on the offer).

We continued to promote the "Integrated Digital Practice" for some years and whilst the name of the company has now changed, it is still core to the message of Carestream Dental.

The whole concept of display advertising is that if you have something different from your competitors you really need to tell everyone about it.

The advertisement below was for a tour we did showing all the products and how they seamlessly integrated with each other

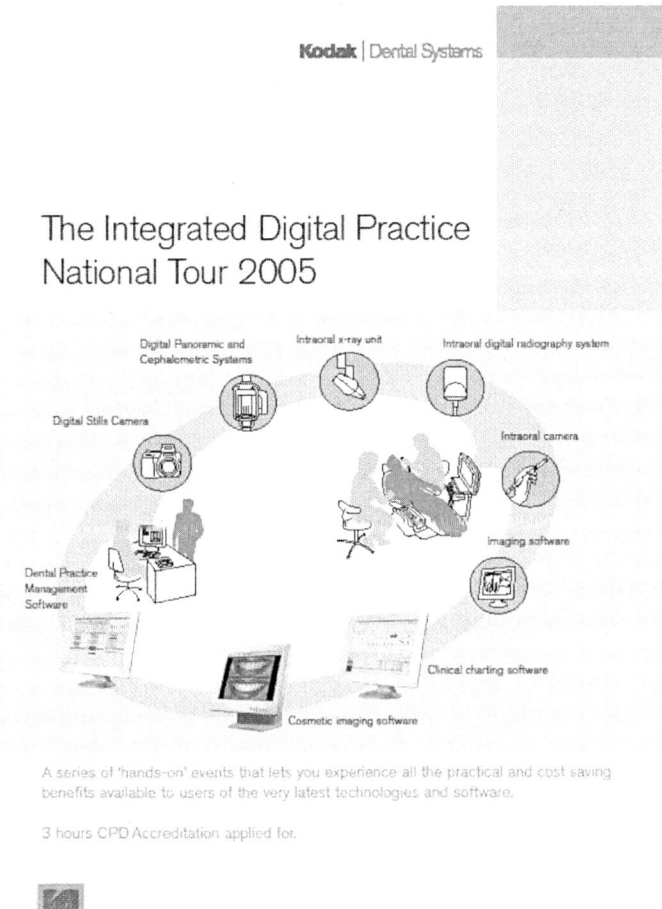

The Integrated Office Ad 2005

So we continued to grow the business very quickly until in 2007 Kodak sold its "Health Group" to a company called Onex and as we were part of the "Health Group", the new company became known as Carestream Health. We were no longer part of Kodak so we had to re-brand again as we could no longer call ourselves "Kodak Dental Systems".

After some discussion we decided that the best course of action would be to revert back to the old name PracticeWorks and for the next three years I concentrated on building this brand again, although this was made doubly difficult because we still called our products "Kodak Dental Systems", which ended in lots of customers not really knowing who we were, this confusion continues to this day.

In 2010 the corporation decided that we had to rebrand again under the name Carestream Dental. As I write this, the re-branding issue is still going on.

Over the last few years as well as being head of Business Development, Sales and Marketing for Carestream in the UK and Ireland, I have been a member of the "Global Marketing Council" for Carestream Dental that is now a global company with annual revenues in excess of $500m.

So from taking my original company from zero to a UK company turning over more than twenty million dollars per year, I have decided to start again and share my experience with the dental profession. My new company Dental Marketing Expert hit the streets in January 2012 www.dentalmarketingexpert.co.uk

Chapter Four
Marketing in the Dental Profession

Lets cut to the chase, is marketing in the dental sector any different from marketing in any other sector? Well basically the answer is an emphatic NO.

If you think that your patients are any different from any other consumer of goods think again, basically you are chasing their hard earned cash just like everyone else is. You have to compete with this year's holiday, a new car, or even whether we go to the cinema or theatre this week.

The fact that you have a degree and you are a professional means little if nothing to the average consumer. Very few people actually enjoy going to the dentist, even if you have the most modern facilities in your area. To the patient (customer) they are going to feel pain and the experience will not be good.

The press are not particularly helpful, we've all seen the headlines of "Greedy Dentist's deserting the NHS" and the inflated prices of getting your teeth seen to.

So based on that prefix, not only are you chasing the same pound in your customer's/patient's pocket, as the local carpet shop, furniture shop, even supermarket. The average person would rather visit most of these establishments rather than your practice.

We know that 50% of the population never sees a dentist and you don't have to be a genius to work out why really. The perception of going to the dentist is (a) its going to hurt and (b) it's going to hurt my pocket. So let's not pretend you don't have to sell to your market unless you are very lucky and happen to have a very loyal patient base who love coming to your practice.

So what's the best strategy, well unfortunately there isn't a single best strategy, you have to try what works for you and test, test, test.

If you send out a local mailer and it doesn't work that doesn't necessarily mean that local mailers don't work, it may well mean that individual mailer didn't work. Equally if you send one out and its successful, it doesn't always mean that if you send it out again it will have the same success. The basic rule of marketing is that everything changes all the time and in 2011 the changes happen faster than ever, where even full time professionals like myself struggle to keep up with every twist and turn.

There are many ways to reach out to your target audience, some of them are below:

- In Surgery/Practice marketing
- Word of Mouth
- TV/Radio
- Local newspapers
- Local magazines
- Specialist magazines
- Yellow Pages
- Local Directories
- Leaflets
- Telesales
- The Web
- Social Media
- Email
- Leaflet drops

- Text Messages
- Direct Mail
- Collaborative Marketing

And just when you thought you knew them all and were starting to get to grips with one or all of these different strategies, along comes a new one.

So as I said earlier there is not one way to address your market, you can literally spend thousands of pounds on what could be a total waste.

One of the biggest mistakes those marketeers make is not testing how different campaigns work. The local press will call you and say they are offering space in the press this week and they only have a few spaces left, so you place and advert. Do you then check how that advert worked? Do you ask how much extra revenue it brought in?

Don't worry most other companies don't either, they see marketing and advertising as a cost and not an investment. Even large companies like the one's I have worked for usually set a budget at the beginning of the year and fix how much they will spend on marketing.

Do you see how misguided that approach is? If they really tested their marketing and tracked what extra revenue it brought in they would never set a budget.

For example lets say that we decide to spend £10,000 per year on marketing, we start our campaign and hey presto we increase revenue by £50,000. Should we stop at that point because we've spent our allocation or should we invest another £10,000 and maybe produce another £50,000? I know what I think, although I could never persuade my superiors in the corporate world to follow this course.

A better way of deciding how much you should spend is to work out how much each customer is worth to you and what their life time spend is with you.

If you asked most people how you would increase your revenues/ profits, they would say we need to increase the number of customers we have.

That isn't necessarily the whole truth; there are actually three factors that will make your company/practice more profitable, that is (a) The number of customers (b) The average transaction value (c) The frequency of purchase.

Here's something I'd like to share with you:

If you currently have 1000 customers with an average spend of £100 your annual turnover will be £100,000, so if you increase your customer base by 10% you will quite rightly increase your turnover by 10%.

However if you could increase the number of customers by 10% the average transaction value by 10% and the frequency of purchase you increase your annual revenue by 30%. This would in effect double your revenues.

So lets discuss that a little further, lets say for instance you see your patient/customer once a year, if you could see them twice a year, you could effectively double your income without taking on another patient.

Or when they come to see you for a check up you get them to see the hygienist or Oral Educator you increase your average transaction value.

Or even more simply you sell an electric tooth brush to 10% of your existing patients etc. etc. etc.

None of this is rocket science, its basic common sense which anyone can adopt. But the vast majority of companies out there do not implement these strategies. One of the best companies who operate up-selling is McDonalds and lets face it the average person selling you your Big Mac is not a natural marketer.

I'm assuming that most people at some time have eaten in a McDonalds, you go up to the counter and you ask for your burger or whatever it is you want. The first thing the person behind the counter says to you is "would you like large, a Meal Deal and large coke". Simply by doing this McDonalds have managed to increase their average transaction value by more than 50% very clever, you can also do this.

This technique is called "Cross Selling" and the very best time to do this is when you're selling something else. Once your customer has gone you've lost the opportunity, you should do this every time you deal with a customer/patient.

And just to be technical this is slightly different to "Up Selling" whereby you sell something more expensive than that you are currently offering. Its very effective, however you have to believe that what you're selling is the right thing to do.

When you think about your patients/customers and your marketing plans you need to think in terms of how much each patient/customer is worth to you.

Most people when they think about the success or failure of a marketing campaign tend to think about how much immediate revenue the campaign delivers. For instance if you charge £50.00 for an examination and an advertisement generates 10 new patients this would equate to £500, but if the advert costs £500 you only break even.

You need to think about the lifetime value of your customer/patient so if that same advertisement which cost you £500, but over the next five years those same ten patients/customers have two examinations per year the actual revenue is not £500 but £5,000 making the cost of your advertisement look quite small in comparison.

Chapter Five
In Practice Marketing

Some time ago when I was visiting one of our customers I was sat in the waiting room and on the table was a Flip Board showing what treatments the dentist did and a large section was dedicated to Implants.

As I flipped my way through the content I was somewhat shocked to see very graphic pictures of implant procedures, blood, bone etc. and all. Now I have seen lots of implant procedures on many occasions, but I don't think I have ever thought wow that looks like a fun thing to do.

Eventually the dentist saw me and I mentioned that I'd noticed he did implants and he enthusiastically confirmed that this was the case. "Do you do many" I asked. "No not many at all really" he replied.

I pointed out his flip chart in the waiting room and asked what he thought of it and he described how it was very informative etc. showing the patient exactly what happens when they have an implant.

I told him that if he wanted to show patients exactly what the procedure would entail, he should maybe use diagrams rather than full colour photographs, because the purpose of the flip chart is not only to inform but also to encourage patients to ask about the facility, he said he would consider my advice.

The point I'm making is that whilst advertising/marketing should always be factual and should never mislead, you should also remember that you are selling a product or service too and that you need to show what would appeal to the customer/patient e.g. an improved smile etc.

I can never understand why the dental waiting room is normally stocked with very out of date magazines and little else. This is the ideal time to market to your patients. They are sat waiting to see you on your premises and you should take every opportunity to introduce them to your services.

Without plugging any particular system, one of the best waiting room marketing tools is PIC from Medivision, this is very similar to a PowerPoint presentation that automatically repeats its self over and over.

Its pretty low tech, it really only needs a flat screen television and an old computer to run it, the cost is a few hundred pounds, you can tailor it to suit your self, use video or animations etc.

So if you do whitening tell them about it and show them before and after results, the same for orthodontics or any form of cosmetic dentistry, you need to sell what you do.

If you put it on the wall I guarantee that your patients will watch it and some of them will ask you about what they have just seen.

If you're not creating a practice newsletter, start tomorrow. Instead of putting a pile of old magazines on the table put your newsletter there. It only needs to be a sheet of A3 folded in two, showing your patients your latest innovations. If you've just invested in digital x-ray, intraoral camera's, 3D imaging, a new decontamination room etc. You need to tell your patients about this, they are interested believe me.

And whilst you're doing that tell them about the different procedures you can do for them.

If necessary show them what your new technology does and how it works.

Every piece of literature you have in the waiting room should be about you, your team and what services you provide and how that can benefit your patients.

If you go to purchase a new car, furniture, carpet, TV etc. you wouldn't expect to read an old magazine would you? There would be lots of brochures on the latest model car etc. It's no different in the dental waiting room.

If you have a web site you need to put the web address on every single piece of stationery you give to the patient. This would include your newsletter, reminder cards and letter heads. Having the most fantastic web site in the world is no use whatsoever if nobody sees it (we'll cover that topic later).

Your web site address should be prominent everywhere in the surgery, so if you are putting a sign with your logo on it somewhere, make sure the web site address is there too.

For the more adventurous of you, you might want to put QR codes on your literature.

These are fairly new and are scanned by mobile devices such as the iPhone and Android smart phones. Once scanned the code takes the user to a section of your web site, or to a video, or

This code links to my web site

pretty much anything you want them to see. You don't see many at the moment but just watch this space, within a couple of years they'll be everywhere. You could steal a march on your competitors.

Just remember this in-practice marketing is great, but if you don't have any patients there it doesn't really cut it!

Chapter Six
Word of Mouth

Word of mouth is incredibly important and can literally make or break a business especially a local one. I have to stress that the very best person to sell/market the practice is (a) You and (b) Happy and contented patients.

Referrals are without doubt the best way you can increase your business turnover.

Just think about anything you choose to buy. You can have the best marketing campaign in the world and maybe the best product too, but if someone you trust says they had a bad experience with it what are you likely to do?

On the other hand if you see something that might not jump off the page at you but a friend or member of the family raves about it, I guarantee you will take much more notice about it.

Let me tell you a true story of something that happened in our office a couple of years ago.

A colleague and I were looking at some before and after photographs of diastema on the cosmetic imaging software we sold at the time.

As we were talking about it, a female colleague saw what we were looking at and asked how the gap in between the two front teeth had been closed, we duly told her. She was quite amazed that this type of treatment could be done, but said no more about the subject and carried on with whatever it was she was doing.

Now I have to say that I'm probably not the most observant person in the world (I'm sure my wife would testify to that) so I would have never thought she had a gap between her front teeth (but she did).

Without mentioning anything to us she saw her dentist and asked if he could close the (almost none existent) gap between her front teeth, he duly told her that yes he could do this.

Some time later she proudly came up to me and gave me a massive smile and asked if I noticed anything different. Now as I said earlier I'm not the most observant person in the world and initially I didn't notice anything, so she told me what she had done, to which I said of course you look fabulous.

She went on to tell me that all her life she had been conscious of the gap between her front teeth and could never smile properly, always masking her upper incisors with her top lip.

I think she paid around £1,500 for the procedure and thought it was the best investment she had ever made.

The point I'm trying to make is that her dentist had been doing this type of treatment for years, she'd also been a patient of his for years, but he had failed to communicate properly with her. As a result she had no idea it could be done and so never asked.

It's your responsibility to communicate what you can do for your patients; in this case it changed her life.

You can also guess what sort of testimonial she would give her dentist if anyone asked can't you!

At every stage you need to be getting feed back from your patients as to what their experience has been. The (Care Quality Commission) CQC regulations now mandate that you have to have some sort of patient survey in place, but rather than be forced into this you should be embracing it at every stage and acting upon it.

You might think all your patients are very happy with you and your practice, whereas actually they may have a very different opinion. Or the opposite might be the case, you will never know unless you offer your patients confidential surveys.

There is a new product just coming on the market as I write this, being marketing by Carestream Dental and Medivision, which is a web based patient survey, it gives brilliant statistics telling you exactly what your patients think about you, your practice and your staff, there may be other products you can buy that do something similar by the time this book reaches you, but you should invest in something like this.

It takes forever to build up a good reputation and this can be destroyed literally overnight (especially with the advent of Facebook and Twitter). Most of you work in a local area, people talk, there are local Facebook groups etc. You must know what your patients think about you and your practice.

You might be the most caring and skilful dentist, but if your staff at the front desk or your hygienist is not giving the best service, this can seriously damage your wealth and once a patient starts to think negatively about you, it's very difficult, if not impossible, to turn them around.

I alluded to Facebook and Twitter, this is a new form of word of mouth, you can't control it, it has a life of its own and word of mouth can spread like wildfire with these two mediums.

Just look at some of the conflicts around the world, quite often the most up to date news from these war zones are by someone tweeting a message about it or putting something on Facebook.

Only the other day the news headlines proclaimed a famous store had to take two T-Shirts off their shelves within hours of putting them on because several customers took offence and tweeted about them, the story made the breakfast news that day.

So do you have a referral strategy in place, do you routinely encourage your patients to refer other people to you? If not, start today.

Ask all your patients if they would be happy to refer a family member or friend to your practice, if they say no, well you're then getting some feed back, if yes then its free marketing.

Use your practice management system to track where your patients are coming from and particularly if they're coming as a referral from another patient, you should be able to see who your best referrers are, reward them, they are great advocates for you.

If you need to reward your patients/customers then do it today. I can't stress just how important it is for you to have referrals they are without doubt the best way to gain new patients who will stay loyal to you.

Chapter Seven
TV, Radio and Video

It goes without saying that one of the most effective forms of marketing are TV and Radio, it also goes without saying that TV and Radio are without doubt the most expensive forms of marketing.

For the vast majority of the people reading this book, my guess is that you will probably never do any TV advertising simply because of the cost. Simply getting an advert made is incredibly expensive, although that said with the vast amount of new channels coming on stream that is changing very quickly

I have to admit that because I have primarily been involved in Business to Business marketing I don't have a great deal of experience in producing TV advertisements although I have produced several promotional videos for the various companies I have been involved with.

Local Radio or even national radio advertising might be something that you should consider, again it is fairly expensive but you can reduce the cost if you advertise outside the most popular times, but for obvious reasons you will reach a smaller audience.

Producing a radio advertisement is relatively easy, unless you are a natural speaker with a voice that comes across well on radio I would recommend you hire a professional person who does this sort of thing; you could probably hire someone to record an advert for around £500.00

You will need to produce a script for the actor/actress to record for you and I would recommend that if you are going to go to the expense of a radio advert, you should have some sort of offer to drive individuals to you such as free examination for first time customers etc. or 20% off whitening etc.

Simply telling people who you are and where your business is. doesn't really cut it and, because of the cost, you need to make sure that your adverts hit the spot every time.

Having said all that there are other cunning ways to use the media. Most local BBC radio stations are desperate for content as they are mandated to have a certain amount of speech every day.

If you contact your local BBC radio station it is highly likely that they will interview you on your opinions of the state of NHS dentistry, how private dentists are being maligned etc. etc. The point is that if you have something to say, you have credibility this is absolutely great marketing.

Guess what is the second biggest search engine in the world today after Google……. Well its You Tube (incidentally owned by Google). You Tube is without doubt the biggest broadcaster in the world and nobody really knows it, forget all the large US channels and the BBC, its You Tube believe me.

You Tube has some absolutely mind blowing statistics as to the number of people it touches. I first read these figures in disbelief.

• More than 13 million hours of video were uploaded during 2010 and 48 hours of video are uploaded every minute, resulting in nearly 8 years of content uploaded every day.

- Over 3 billion videos are viewed a day
- Users upload the equivalent of 240,000 full-length films every week
- More video is uploaded to You Tube in one month than the 3 major US networks created in 60 years
- 70% of You Tube traffic comes from outside the US

You Tube Screen Shot

I could go on but I think you will agree that the statistics are amazing; most TV stations would give their right arm for these numbers.

But you can join in with this and making your own promotional video has never been easier or cheaper and you can distribute it with ease on You Tube. There is one little problem though - you need your customers to see it and in order to do this you need to optimise your video just as you should optimise your web site too. This can be a daunting exercise and you might be advised to get a professional to help you do this.

Optimisation is effectively making what you put on the web "Search Engine Friendly". It is quite a complex subject based around key words, links, click through rates etc. and probably needs a book simply to cover this subject. In fact you can buy "Search Engine Optimisation For Dummies" for just over £15.00 from Amazon if you really want to get savvy in this field.

Chapter Eight
Local Newspaper, Magazine, Yellow Pages

For years this has been the traditional way to advertise your company/practice and it is still reasonably effective.

Lets talk about local newspapers first. These publications are usually produced on a weekly basis, in many cases they are delivered free to addresses in the area.

The prices for advertising in these publications are quite reasonable, but you have to remember that you are competing with just about every single business that is also operating in your area.

There are two basic types of advertising the first is display advertising, this is where you buy space in the publication and the bigger space you want, the more you pay.

Just as with local radio advertising, I would recommend that if you are going to take out a display advert, you should have something different to tell your potential customers/patients.

It doesn't always need to be a special offer although this helps; you could for instance advertise that you have installed some really fabulous equipment, software or cameras etc that will make your practice more advanced than other practices in your area.

So for instance if you have recently purchased a new intraoral camera, put an advertisement in telling the public that in your practice you use the most advanced techniques and that they can see everything on a large in-surgery screen.

Or if you invest in a 3D scanner, tell them how this will make your practice even safer for them.

As with any marketing you need to think about what it is that you are trying to achieve. Is it to grow your business generally or get new patients for a new hygienist, dentist, oral educator etc. or you may have recently qualified for a specialist area such as implants?

If you have a new hygienist for instance you could run an advert saying that for first 100 new patients you will give them a 30% discount on their hygienist appointment.

This won't cost you a great deal and should generate many new patients.

I would recommend that if you are going to run advertisements in the local press, where you are giving something away, you print some sort of code that the patient can bring with them. This does two things firstly it will encourage the patient to act on the offer as everyone likes this type of thing and secondly it makes it measurable for you as you can see exactly how many new patients the campaign delivered.

The second is of course classified, this has been a great way of getting your business noticed for a very small investment over the years and it is still the case today. But as with display advertising make sure you have something to say rather than just state your practice or business name.

Here's another tip too don't pick one advertisement and book two months of advertising, put one add in for a couple of weeks and then try something different, keep testing the response.

Yellow Pages was,without doubt, the best medium for local businesses to advertise themselves. That status has now changed and the best place is the Internet (we'll discuss that later), however the good old Yellow Pages still has a place.

Yellow Pages excelled because unlike a display advert or classified ad in the press, the customer is actively looking for your service not simply reading an article and noticing an advert on the page.

For instance if a local garage takes out an advertisement in the local paper and you happen to see it, it will only be of interest to you if you actually need a garage at that time. Whereas with Yellow Pages you specifically look for the service or product you require.

The basic listing is free as soon as a company applies for a telephone number; all businesses are entitled to their free slot. The prices for display advertising are pretty reasonable too.

Home Improvements

ANTON PAVING CO. LLC
Old Lyme 860-434-5211
(See display ad on page 187)

COTTAGE CARE CONSTRUCTION ~ Damian Ranelli
43 Chapman Beach Road, Westbrook 860-399-4745
(See display ad on inside back cover)

MOODUS ELECTRIC LLC
Joshua Becker ~ Electrical Contractor, Moodus 860-873-8848
(See display ad on page 185)

SAYLES RESTORATION ~ Commercial & Residential
Madison ....203-245-2205 or 203-815-7577
(See display ad on page 196)

TOP NOTCH ELECTRICAL SERVICES LLC
24 Anderson Lane, Deep River.. 860-526-3960
(See display ad on page 185)

Indoor Playground

ABC'S GYMNASTICS STARS
40 Industrial Park Road, Niantic.. 860-691-1235
(See display ad on page 187)

189

Typical Yellow Pages Advertisements

56

If you are going to have a display advertisement in the Yellow Pages don't make the mistake that the vast majority of businesses advertising in there make. They simply put their name or the name of their business in bold type with their contact details, you will have seen dozens like this and what is the point?

Just look at the large advert at the bottom of the page above, they've obviously paid for a large display advertisement, and given it a little thought, but the biggest line is their name which means nothing to us, and the fact that they're a "Friendly Insurance Agency" does that cut it for you?

When a potential customer is looking through the Yellow Pages for a local dentist and they see a name in bold type, why would they choose that one rather than the one directly under it with their name in bold?

The same applies to any other business they all think that by simply displaying their name, they will attract customers (why?). Unless someone has told you about that company or dental practice what would drive you to contact them?

If you're going to pay for an advert you should say something different to your competitors such as "We Use The Latest Technology To Make Our Practice Safer" or "We specialise in treating nervous patients". It really doesn't matter what you put so long as it makes you appear to be different. You need to jump out of the page and grab their attention, the headline is everything.

Chapter Nine
Leaflets

Leaflet drops are a much-maligned activity and very few dental practices use this media.

Using this form of marketing is (a) cheap (b) very targeted (c) very informative for the customer (d) has a high success rate. For instance, if you were to do the very same campaign but use direct mail instead your costs would increase substantially. By the time you have printed your letter, inserted it in an envelope and put a stamp on the envelope, you are probably looking at around £1.00 for every letter.

On the other hand you can have leaflets printed to a very high quality. Your cost of delivery could literally be zero if you do it yourself, or you could ask one of the local newsagents to deliver it for you, this is normally very cheap. Royal Mail, in some areas, also provide this service - again, it's certainly worth an enquiry phone call.

We are all accustomed to receiving leaflets from the local Indian, Chinese, Fish and Chip restaurants etc. and if you are like me you often keep at least one of each so you know where to go the next time you fancy a take away. So why not the local dentist?

Again if you are going to go to the trouble of having something like this printed make sure you have something different to say, don't just put your name and the fact that your are a local dentist, tell them something they will be interested in or have some sort of special offer.

Chapter Ten
Telesales

Telesales is a highly targeted and effective form of marketing, however I would be very careful about using this form of advertising to generate new customers as you will effectively be conducting "Cold Calling" and not everyone appreciates companies calling them with sales messages out of the blue.

Cold Calling via the telephone is much more effective if you are engaged in business to business activity, as you can call during working hours when most people are not too offended if you call them about some sort of promotion that you are running.

That said if you are trying to generate more business a great source is your practice management software and your existing patient list.

You can use the telephone to speak to patients who might not have been to see you for more than a year, or even to patients who see you regularly but have not had a hygienist appointment, or seen the oral educator etc.

If you are going to have an open day for the practice, for instance, running a telesales campaign to get your patients to come in is very effective, because they will not see you as just trying to sell them something, you are their dentist or have been at some time or other.

Incidentally whilst we're on the topic, the vast majority of dentists do not use their practice management software for marketing purposes either at all, or very sparingly. This is a magic source of revenue for you; quite literally it is an untapped gold mine.

You have the names, addresses, email addresses, telephone numbers of everyone who has visited your practice since you installed the system and you should value it.

You should be able to run reports on, it that will show you exactly who hasn't had an appointment for more than a year. Tqqhen call them with some form of offer to come back and see you, it doesn't have to be hard sales, simply one of your reception staff calling everyone with a friendly greeting and telling them about something you are doing. You'll be amazed how effective this can be.

If you don't have the staff or time to do this you can employ a telesales agency that will run a campaign for you on a cost per call basis. I have been using this method for years now and it is one of the most effective forms of marketing I have employed. You can see the results of the campaign immediately and usually find out a lot of extra information too.

Chapter Eleven
The Web

Many companies, in fact most companies, think of their web site as something different to their (proper) business and I mean large companies too.

Your web site should be integral not just with your other marketing but your whole business strategy. If it isn't the most important part of your communications with your public, it soon will be.

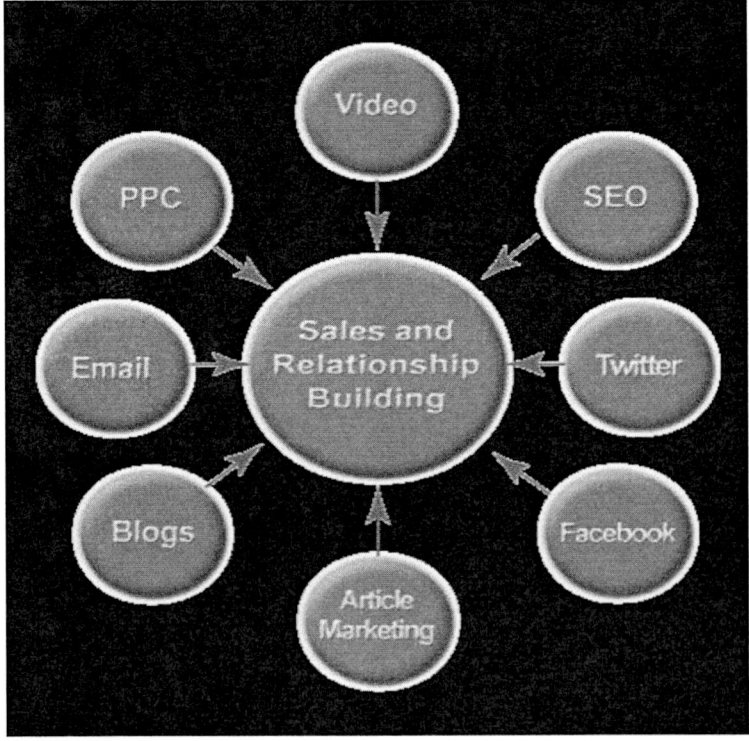

Your web site is integral to everything you do on the world wide web it needs to integrate with all the other elements of e-marketing, including Pay Per Click, Video, Search Engine Optimisation, Twitter, Facebook, Article Marketing, Blogs Email etc.

I'm going to be somewhat controversial here and say this. "Great Web Site Design Does NOT Increase Business". A great web site might make you feel better about yourself. It might impress your friends and family. It might even impress your patients, it will almost certainly impress your web site designer, but it will seldom if ever increase revenues on its own.

Just let me emphasise my point. Who has the most recognisable web site on the planet, look below.

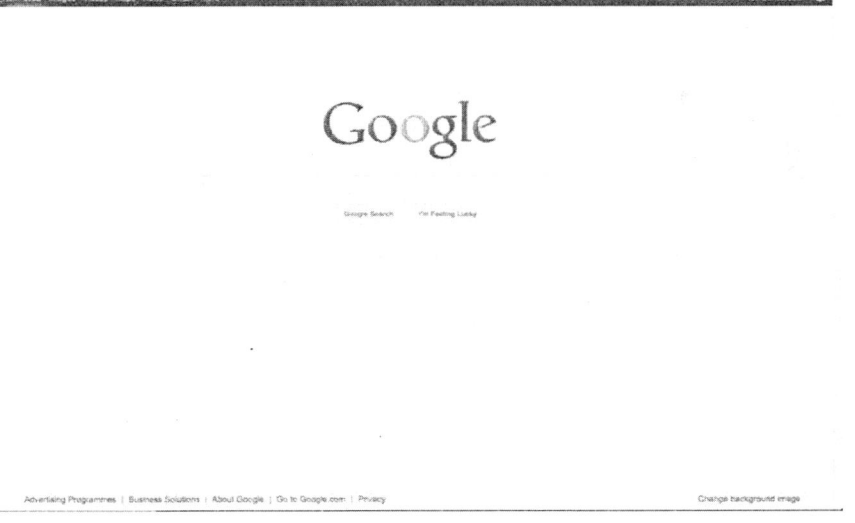

Now if you'd been one of the Venture Capitalists that Larry Page and Sergey Brin (now multi billionaires) went to with their idea of starting

Google and showed you the above web page as the bed rock of their company, do you think you would have given them the money?

It's no mistake that just about every Google page is either very simple or downright ugly and yet they manage to make in excess of $20bn every year.

Look at most web sites, certainly the dental variety of which some are very well designed. They are really just attempting to be shop windows. Unfortunately as they are not on a high street they are actually somewhere else and very few, if anyone, can find them.

If you want to see brilliant web presence, look no further than Amazon. Just about any product you search for will appear in the search listing if Amazon stock it and that's no accident. They are, without doubt, the benchmark for e-marketing of any company on the planet, just look at the Google search below. I was looking for a video camera and look who comes top of the list, in both paid for search and generic search. *(Paid search is the top result highlighted in yellow and the sites down the right hand side of the page. Generic search are all the other sites below the top one highlighted in yellow).*

And when I get to the page everything I want is there, making it so easy for me to buy the product in seconds. If I want I can have a full technical description of the product. There are customer reviews; I can buy it new or second hand and from a variety of suppliers. This is a real no frills brilliant site for buying stuff; they know exactly what they want to do and ruthlessly achieve it.

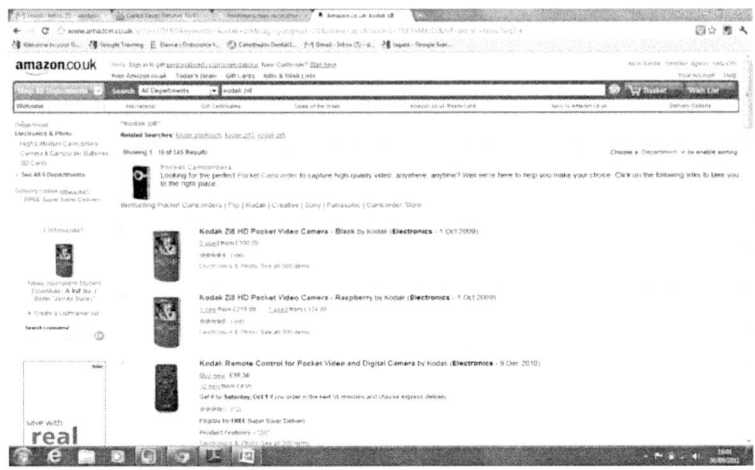

Amazon's Brilliant Web Pages

Unfortunately most of us don't have the resources of Amazon and probably never will. Sadly statistics show that 99% of people who visit a web site not only don't buy anything, they never do anything either, such as register their name or book an appointment etc. don't you think that's incredible, 99%? The average amount of time that most people spend on a web site is eight seconds. So does your web site pass the eight-second test?

Just look at your web site as you would any other site when you are surfing the web. What would make you stay on the site if you didn't already know the company?

Most companies, dental or otherwise, have absolutely no idea how long people stay on their site, which pages they visit, what the last page they were on before they left was, so why even have a web site?

There are literally billions of web sites and the number is increasing every day so if you are going to have a web site, you need to think about what you want it to do and how potential customers are going to find it.

So lets talk about what it is you want to achieve from a web site, do you want to attract new patients, talk to your existing customers, do you want to explain what services you offer, how big you are, are you looking for lead generation, to make sales etc?

To achieve any of the above the first thing you need to do is make sure that people can find your web site and that usually means making sure that Google can find you. In the US Google has around 65% of the market with Yahoo and Bing sharing most of what's left. In the UK Google has 95% of the market so you really want to be optimised for Google above any other search engine.

There are two ways that Google can find you. The first way is by generic search, which tries to find the best results that people enter when they search for something. Google refers to this as relevance and they are obsessed by this, above everything else.

Effectively the content of your site must be relevant to the person who is looking for your service or goods. If Google doesn't serve up relevant sites to your search eventually you will move to another search provider and they don't want that.

This usually means you have to deploy Search Engine Optimisation (SEO) in order to be at the top of the first page in the search; most people searching for a product or service never go to the bottom of page one let alone page two.

The problem with SEO is that Google keeps moving the goal posts regarding the criteria it is looking for and they keep it a secret anyway, so experts in the SEO field are constantly trying to second guess what Google wants to see all the time.

You may find that you are top of the list on page one of Google when someone enters a search, only to find that tomorrow you are somewhere on page three or four, this can be catastrophic to a business who relies on the web for new business.

Allegedly the best way to ensure that you will be top of the list and on page one of the generic searches in Google, is to have lots of other web sites linking to yours, but this is very difficult to achieve and they may change this at any time assuming its what they want in the first place.

There are other ways too, such as using key words in your site and content, which is becoming more important to Google, along with video, all of which can be optimised for the search engines.

To employ a Search Engine Specialist can be very expensive and as I said earlier needs to be constantly monitored and tweaked. You could study the subject yourself and try and make your Web Site Google friendly. See my reference to "Search Engine Optimisation For Dummies" earlier.

The other route to drive traffic to your site is using Pay Per Click (PPC). This is literally what it says you set up an account with Google and you pay for advertising.

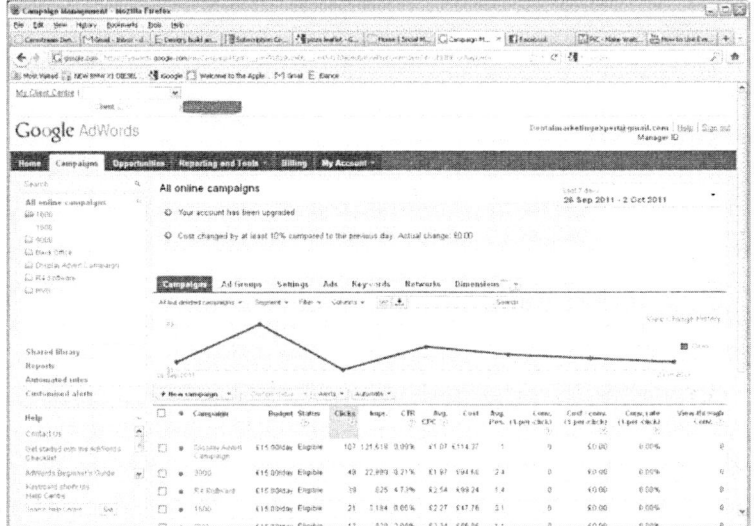

Adwords Account Screen

If you have ever done a search on Google, you will notice that there are usually three top sites on the page display being highlighted on the left and a list of other sites down the right hand side of the page, these are all sponsored links or paid for displays.

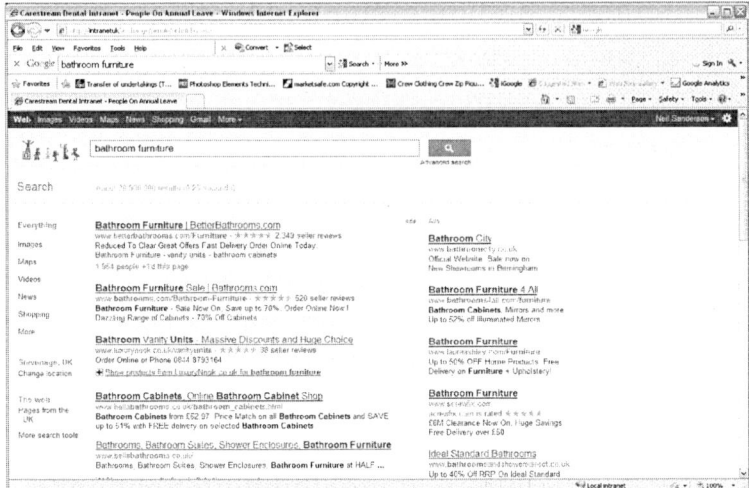

Google Search Screen

This form of advertising is probably the best thing that has happened for advertisers. Just compare an advert in the local newspaper to a paid for advert on Google.

The newspaper will first of all ask you to pay up front for your advert. The advert will duly be printed and the newspaper may or may not be read by someone who is looking for your services.

It is a scattergun approach, you hope that maybe someone will see your advert and be looking to purchase what you offer.

Google advertising is the complete opposite of this approach; only people who are looking for your services will ever see your advertisement, as it works on key words and location.

So for instance if your business is in Windsor, and you have put in the correct key words and location into your advert, only people who are looking for dentist in Windsor will ever see your placement, so you know you are hitting the correct customers.

And better still you only pay when someone clicks on the link through to your web site.

Now just what they do when they reach your web site is up to you, but you can specify exactly where on your site you want them to arrive (the landing page) and what better page than a "Book and Appointment" page.

Just as with search engine advertising you can also have display adverts with Google (and Bing and Yahoo). This means that your advertisement will be displayed on one of Google's display advertising partners sites, of which there are hundreds of thousands if not millions.

You can design your advert to fit most sizes. You are normally charged on a price per 000 impressions, (this is the number of times your advert has been shown) this effectively means whenever they are displayed to the person surfing the web.

This is a great way to get a message out to lots of people very quickly however it is much more of a scatter gun approach and not as targeted as the search advertising.

Different types of Google Display adverts

We could discuss Search Engine advertising forever. It is quite time consuming to run these campaigns and just like Search Engine Optimisation needs to be constantly tested, tweaked etc. to get the best out of it. But it is the very first thing I would recommend most business try before any other form of advertising, particularly the search version rather than the display.

Studies show that when a person actually arrives at your site, you have around eight seconds to get their attention before they move on. So when you look at your web site what is it that makes it stand out from the others? It needs really catchy headlines just like a newspaper article, that jump out at people and grab their attention. Quite often less is more in this area and sites with many pages may not work as well as a very simple site, with fewer pages depending on what it is you are selling.

But here is a brilliant dental web page, they know exactly what they want and make it incredibly easy for patients to book online.

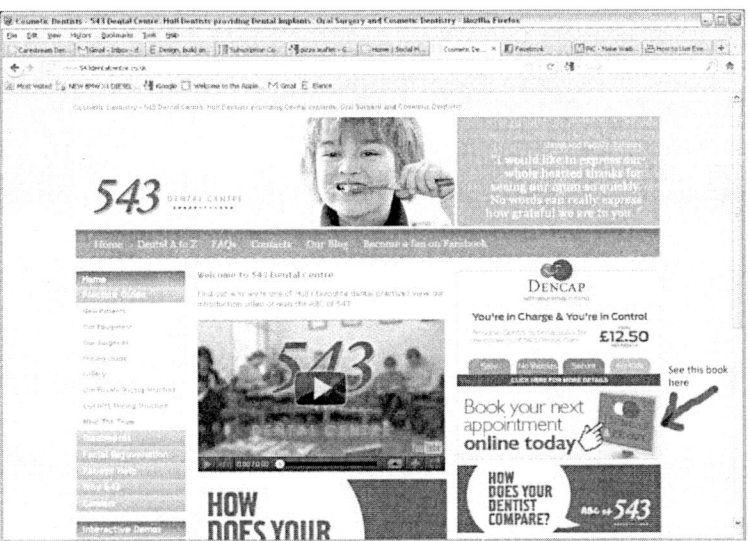

543 Dental's Home Page

This page really jumps out at you, it has a testimonial in the top right hand corner, video in the middle of the page and on the right you can go ahead and book your self an appointment straight away.

And when you get there "online booking"

543 Dental utilises online-booking, I know the practice well and they are one of the most successful practices in Hull.

They make it incredibly easy for their patients and prospective patients to make an appointment (isn't that what we all want?). It's not hidden somewhere on page three, it's right there on the front page "Book Online".

If you don't want to invest in your own web site, you may also want to consider taking a "Google Places" page, these are the sites that appear in a Google search with the little speech bubbles next to them and on a Google Map.

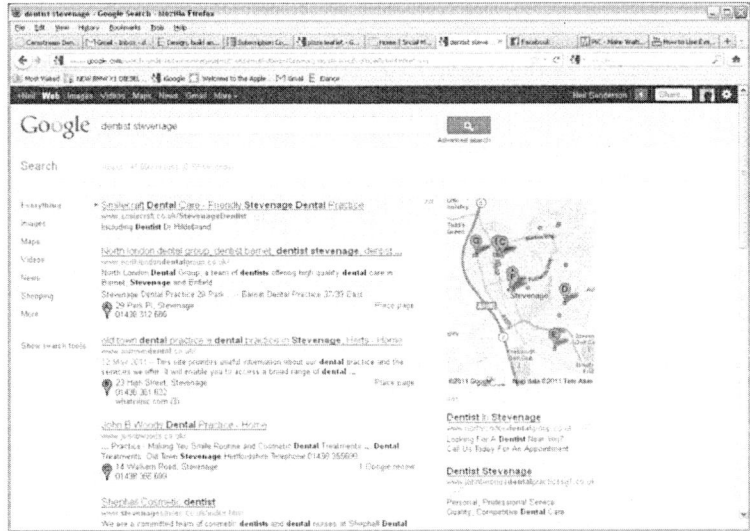

Google Places Page

It is like having another web site, or if you don't already have a web site you can set up a Google Places web site for free. Again it needs optimisation, and one of the best ways to get to the top of the listings is to have lots of good references.

Again Google are looking for relevance and wants to present the best information it can to its users, so it ranks your Google Places site on (amongst other things) references. It is very important that you have as many good references on the site as possible from your patients. Beware though, do not under any circumstances put references there yourself, these must be valid references from real patients/customers. Google is very good at checking this and if you are found out your page will be removed without notice and it is very difficult to get the page back on there.

In addition to references you can put special offers there, vouchers, video, photographs etc. in fact the more information you put there the better as far as Google is concerned and it's completely free.

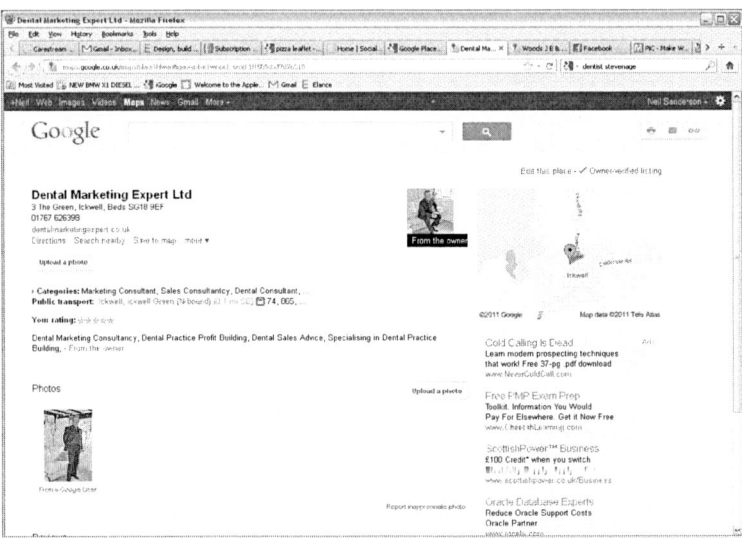

Google Places Web Page

Unfortunately the above is what the vast majority of Google Places pages look like, they have very little information there and it's a real waste of a free space. My excuse is that I hadn't started my business at this point and contractually wasn't allowed put much there.

The big thing is to get your patients to put reviews up on the site, the more reviews you have the higher your ranking will be with Google.

Chapter Twelve
Social Media

Without doubt the buzz word at the moment is Social Media and that generally means the following:

Facebook
Twitter
Blogging
Linkedin
Google+
My Space (although now in decline)
Lots of smaller specialist providers

Whilst I think that every business needs to have a presence in these areas, do not assume that this will build your business on its own. It is very difficult to quantify how, or if, these mediums are working for you. The only people I know who are making lots of money from Social Media are consultants who specialise in this subject.

Social media marketing is very different from just about every other type of marketing, in that you can't really overtly sell (unless you buy advertising space) with one of the providers, which incidentally can be highly targeted (even more than Google adwords), in that you can specify gender, age groups, even down to only people who are engaged or married etc.

However if you don't want to pay for advertising on one of the above you should not overtly sell your services as they are all deemed to be "Social" sites.

For instance you need to view social media like being invited to a dinner party and converse with people as you would at the party. You would never dream of only talking about your business at a dinner party, or if you did you would very quickly run out of friends. Neither would you shout to everyone that you have 50% off teeth whitening this week either.

You should always endeavour to talk about things that are interesting. For instance a member of staff may have had a baby, or is getting married, or just come back from an interesting holiday and maybe occasionally mentioning discretely what offers you may have in the practice.

Ideally you should integrate Social Media with all your other online activities and your web site should be the hub of everything. This is where you can really sell your products and services. All the social media sites should be used to drive traffic to your site.

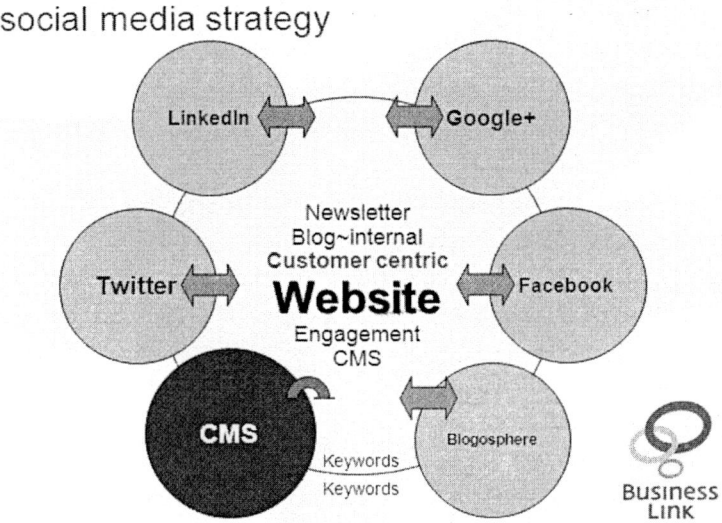

How you should integrate Social Media

Facebook

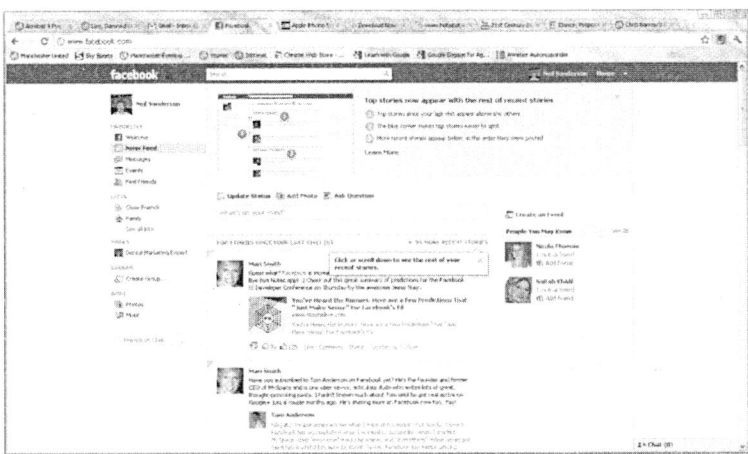

Just as with You Tube there are some incredible statistics for Facebook

- More than 750 million active users (more than 10% of the world's population).
- 50% of active users log on to Facebook in any given day.
- Average user has 130 friends.
- More than 70 translations available on the site
- About 70% of Facebook users are outside the US
- Entrepreneurs and developers from more than 190 countries build with Facebook platform
- Every month, more than 250 million people engage with Facebook on external web sites
- Since social plugins launched in April 2010, an average of 10,000 new websites integrate with Facebook every day
- More than 2.5 million web sites have integrated with Facebook, including over 80 of comScore's US top 100 websites and over half of comScore's global top 100 websites
- There are more than 250 million active users currently accessing Facebook through their mobile devices.
- People that use Facebook on their mobile devices are twice as active on Facebook than non-mobile users.

Quite amazing isn't it, personally I'm not a huge fan of Facebook, or any of the other Social Media sites really, but the statistics show that you can't ignore it as a marketing opportunity.

You can build a page very quickly on Facebook and have your practice have a page too.

Whilst it is effectively free to use Facebook to market your business, you do need to spend time on it, unlike your web site you can't just put it up there and forget about it, you need to be active, which can be very time consuming and it's not something you can just leave to a junior member of staff to deal with.

Twitter

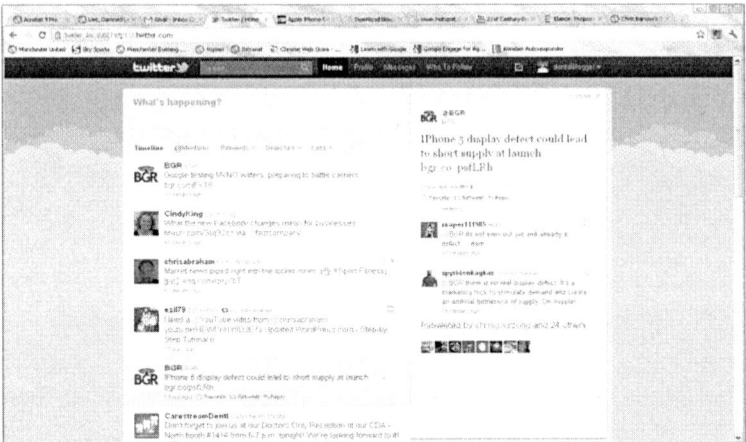

Twitter Screen

For want of a better description Twitter is a bit like text messaging on the internet, in that it is limited to 140 characters. As of today it has in the region of 200 million user's world wide. Twitter is sometimes referred to as Microblogging.

Whilst I am sure that Twitter could be a significant help to the marketer, I have to confess that I am even less enthused with Twitter than I am Facebook.

The concept of the platform is that you send out messages to people in your group (similar to Facebook) and you "follow" other people and receive their "Tweets".

I only follow people who I think are influential in marketing or dentistry etc. but I have to say that the vast majority of "Tweets" I read are so trivial that I really struggle with it. What people are doing today, where they ate last night or whether their flight was on time, doesn't really concern me.

I'm not convinced that Twitter is the marketing medium I would recommend first to the dental industry (or any industry really). It may be OK to tell your best friend where you are, or what you've done, but I'm really not convinced that your patients or customers will want to know that sort of information.

You can now also advertise on Twitter although I have to confess I have never tried it personally.

However I am open minded about the phenomena and try and "Tweet" my followers as and when i think it is necessary.

As with Facebook try and refrain from Tweeting your latest marketing offers as this is an even bigger turn off than hearing what you had for your breakfast.

Blogging
Is a bit like having your own newspaper column in which you can talk about anything you like. But unlike newspapers it doesn't have to have any verified substance (maybe not like newspapers after all). You can put whatever you want in a blog.

It can be as long or as short as you want, there appears to be no average length of a blog. The blog can contain video, photographs as well as words.

Creating a blog is relatively simple and there are web sites around designed specifically for blogging. Probably the best of these sites is Word Press, which is free and has many templates for you to use, as well as lots of plug ins to help you blog.

Once you post a blog on Word Press it effectively makes your blog available for anyone to see and comment on .

Blogging can be an extremely effective way to communicate with your customers and or patients. It can be as long or short as you want it to be. I've tried to ascertain what is the ideal length for a Blog and nobody really seems to know. I would recommend you publish often but keep them fairly short.

The Blog needs to be relevant to your audience although it doesn't need to strictly adhere to the topic you choose to talk about. It really has no boundaries, very similar to Facebook in that respect.

You should encourage your audience to join in and comment on the Blog, this helps create a bond between you and your audience it can also be the source of new ideas. Be prepared though Blog readers can be fairly demanding. So for instance if you write a weekly Blog and for one reason or another miss an edition your audience may well be on your back asking where you are, which can be a tad annoying if you're sat by the pool on your holiday.

As I said earlier Blogging can be a great way to communicate with your audience but it can be very time consuming and even the most creative of writers suffer from writers block now and again.

Linkedin

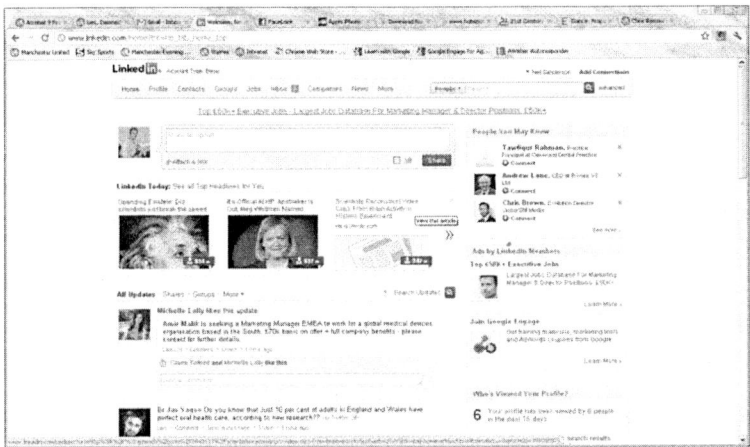

Linkedin Screen

LinkedIn is a bit like Facebook for professionals, as I write this it has 120 million users. I've been with Linkedin for some time now, although for most of that time I was a full time employee of my previous employer so wasn't using it to promote my business

Unlike Facebook where you have friends, Linkedin has links or a contact network. You can invite other users to become part of your network these are called "connections"

Employers can post jobs and search for potential candidates, job seekers can review the profile of the companies they may want to work for.

You can upload you CV and are encouraged to put your professional credentials there, where you are working now, your past employment,what you are good at and the type of thing you would like to do etc.

It's also useful for entrepreneurs to put their business on, which is useful for the likes of me, because I consult to the dental profession. I'm not so sure that it would be of benefit to the average practice owner to increase the number of patients.

I think LinkedIn has great potential for business to business communication and I would encourage all small businesses that deal in this area to become a member of the community.

As with the other social networking sites its free so give it a go, you don't really have anything to lose and it doesn't need as much of your time as Facebook.

Google+

As I write this now I can't tell you a great deal about Google+, it is the new kid on the block and has only just gone live, although it did manage to get itself 25 million users within the first couple of weeks of launch, that's the power of Google.

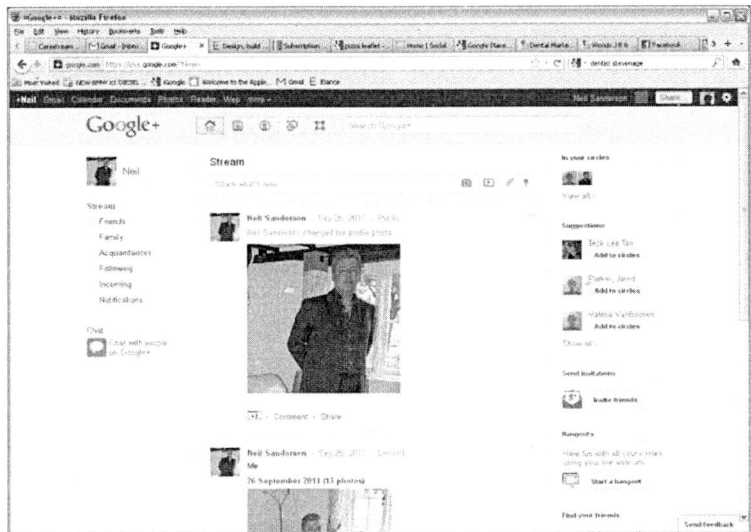

My Google + Page

Google+ is a direct competitor to Facebook; it has some very nice features, which Facebook doesn't have (at the moment) such as circles. Which allow you define what category your friends are, such as close friends, family, work colleagues etc.

I think this concept is very good and reading in between the lines, the guys at Facebook are a little concerned about this new upstart. I suspect a great deal of this concern is down to the fact that it's Google who are muscling in on their space.

My personal view is that within a year Google+ will be a serious competitor to Facebook, let's wait and see.

Myspace

From 2005 to 2008 Myspace was the most visited social networking site in the world. In 2008 Myspace was overtaken by Facebook and ever since then has been in decline. Unless you are in the music business, where it still reigns supreme. It has just announced that this is the area it intends to concentrate on, having lost the battle with Facebook.

If you want to have your business on this type of social media site my recommendation would be to use Facebook. I can't really think of any reason why you would want to have a Myspace account for your business (sorry if I've offended Myspace users).

Chapter Thirteen
Email

Email is a fabulous way to market yourself and your company, however there are good and bad ways to do this. As you can probably testify from your own in-box, we are constantly being bombarded by spammers, that is people or companies who, by one way or another, get your email address and send unsolicited mail.

I'm not saying that every piece of unsolicited email you receive is worthless, but a large amount of it is just that. Really it is no different to the amount of junk mail you receive through the letterbox, some of it is interesting and some of it isn't.

I'm fairly tolerant of Junk Mail and unsolicited email. I have found many useful companies and products via this means of communication. I am one of what is probably the minority of people that would rather receive it and throw away what I don't want, than someone who just blocks it all out, it's just my personal preference.

So how should you conduct an email campaign? Firstly you need to gain the permission of the recipient to send them email and there are many ways of doing this.

Ideally you will already have the email addresses of all your patients, on your dental practice management software. If you make a point of asking your patients if they are OK with you sending them promotional mail, they shouldn't object too much when you send something, so long as you don't bombard them with marketing material all the time.

Most of your patients, whilst maybe not welcoming email from you, will almost certainly read it and not put you in their junk mail list. As with the social media tools, such as Facebook, you can use email to keep in touch with your patients, telling them of events happening in the business etc.

You should always give the recipients of your mail the option to opt out of receiving your mail and make sure that your system has an alert for you not to send email, if they have indicated they don't want to receive them.

E-mails should be short and to the point, just like the type of email you would send to a colleague or friend. If you want to explain in more detail, or show photographs etc., the best way to do this, is to put a link to your web site on it. The busy spam email we all receive is typically full of lots of pictures which really don't do it for me, and I suspect you either.

As well as using email for general marketing promotions, you should also be reminding your patients of their upcoming appointments, along with a text message. You could also thank them for their recent visit. How about sending them a happy birthday greeting.

As a dentist you are in a very privileged position to market to your practice. Most businesses simply don't have the same level of trust with their customers, you have with your patients. So long as you are clever with your marketing and maybe employ the talents of someone like me to advise you, email can be the salvation of your practice; it can build bonds, encourage loyalty and enable you to charge premium prices. Effectively getting you through the worst recession. I can't emphasise how powerful this medium is.

Chapter Fourteen
Text Messaging

Whilst I was responsible for the Sales and Marketing at Carestream Dental, the single biggest frustration I had with our customers was their reluctance to embrace text messaging.

After several years of promoting this means of communication to our customers, only around 30% of dental practices are currently using text messaging

Without doubt text messaging is one of the most powerful marketing tool you have available to you and the majority of dental practices don't use this.

Most marketers would give their hind teeth to get a list of customers mobile numbers, the owners of which would be happy to receive text messages from them.

Before I carry on let me deal with some myths about text messages, I used to hear this all the time:

1. "We call our patients to remind them of their appointment because we like the personal touch" this is without doubt amongst the most misguided statement I've heard. Most of your patients are out during the daytime, so what's the point of calling them! So you leave a message on their answer phone. Please tell me someone, how is that more "personal than sending them a text message"?

2. "We like to write to our patients to remind them of their appointment". Goodness me I really can't believe people actually think this is a better way to communicate. If you are like me, you probably receive six or seven letters through the post every day and most of them get put to one side until I have time to read them, usually at the weekend. It costs a fortune to send stuff through the post and most people don't actually read it, (everyone reads a text message).

3. "Lots of my patients are elderly and don't have a mobile" Oh dear. My mum and mother-in-law are both well into their 70's, so is my dad. They all have a mobile and they all text. My dad doesn't have a computer and can barely use the TV, but he has a mobile phone, this excuse is complete rubbish.

4. "My patients keep changing their mobile number" Just think about this one, are your patients any different to you? When did you last change your mobile number? You might have changed your phone, but you almost certainly kept the same number. A survey was recently carried out by a text messaging provider and even in the

most deprived areas, less than 4% of people changed their mobile number in any five-year period.

So now we've covered the myths let's look at the costs. Most of the practice management software providers' offer a text messaging service and the costs vary between 5p and 10p per text message sent. This is much cheaper than making a phone call and a fraction of the cost of a letter or card.

And guess what? Your patients/customers actually read text messages (you do, don't you?). Without doubt text messages are one of the most powerful tools you have in your itinerary to communicate with your patients and most dentists don't use it at all.

You should be sending every one of your patients a birthday greeting by text, if you know when they got married congratulate them on their anniversary, the same if they've recently had a baby, text a congratulation.

My wife lives and breaths via text, I can never understand why she will spend several hours with her friend and when she gets home, is straight on the mobile texting her, I don't think she is different form most people (OK maybe not me). But don't you get it? All the other means of communicating with your customers/patients are limited to the more traditional methods but you have access to something much more powerful i.e. a mobile number.

So long as you don't become silly about texting, you can market any special offers you have. As I mentioned before congratulate them on their birthday/anniversary etc. It is just a more personal way of contacting your patients and it's this type of communication, that will enable you to keep a loyal patient list, who will get you through these difficult times.

You have all the information you need to do this incredibly powerful marketing in your practice management software, dates of birth, phone numbers, special dates etc. Start using it now.

Chapter Fifteen
Direct Mail

Direct Mail is one of the most effective means of marketing you or any other business can use. It is highly targeted, you can monitor the effectiveness of it very easily and it is relatively inexpensive.

You have probably actively already been using direct mail for many years; you just call it recalling your patients. However there is no reason why you can't use this activity to add some marketing material at the same time.

If you are sending out a card to remind a patient of their appointment, why don't you get them printed with some message or other printed on it?

If you send a letter, send something else with it at the same time. Maybe a promotion for tooth whitening etc, this is a great opportunity to get some sort of message across.

There is one huge advantage that you as a dental professional has over just about any other business and that is you know the dates of birth of all your customers. Just look at this card I received the other day from the company that sold me my car a year ago.

JOY CELEBRATES ANNIVERSARIES.

CELEBRATE THE 1ST ANNIVERSARY OF YOUR BMW WITH A £25 VOUCHER TOWARDS AN EXCLUSIVE DINING EXPERIENCE.

Front view of the BMW card

CELEBRATE THE 1ST ANNIVERSARY OF YOUR BMW PURCHASE WITH SPECIALIST CARS AND DINE AT THE BLACK HORSE, IRELAND OR THE BIRCH, WOBURN.

As a small token of our appreciation, Specialist Cars in association with The Black Horse, Ireland and The Birch, Woburn are delighted to offer you £25 towards a meal when you dine in either of these fantastic restaurants.

This exclusive offer is open to Specialist Cars customers as an appreciation of your business and a celebratory experience of your 1st anniversary of owning your BMW. Simply present this voucher to a member of staff prior to ordering your meal, and you will receive £25* towards your bill.

The Black Horse
Ireland, Near Shefford
Bedfordshire SG17 5QL
01462 811398
www.blackhorseireland.com

The Birch
20 Newport Road, Woburn
Bedfordshire MK17 9HX
01525 290295
www.birchwoburn.com

Issue No. 150737
Issue Date: 12·10·11
Expiry Date: 12·01·12

Specialist Cars Tring
01442 890666 www.specialistcarsbmwtring.co.uk

Specialist Cars Luton
01582 590700 www.specialistcarsbmwluton.co.uk

Specialist Cars Stevenage
01438 760200 www.specialistcarsbmwstevenage.co.uk

*Offer available at the restaurants detailed above. Offer valid until the date stated. This offer is exclusive of the month of December and all promotional offers or special events. The amount can only be used against meals of 2 or more.

Rear view of BMW card

They sent me this on the anniversary of the purchase of my car. They are offering me £25.00 off the price of a meal at one of my favourite restaurants in the area.

(Incidentally if you are ever in Bedfordshire with some time on your hands, try out the Black Horse in Ireland, it's a fabulous restaurant).

Now I don't suppose for one minute that Specialist Cars are paying the full £25.00, they are almost certainly working hand in hand with the restaurant, which I am sure would like to attract BMW drivers to their establishment.

The big selling point is that they appeared to remember exactly when I bought the car (was probably just generated from a computer), and sent me a free gift. Whilst they are not going to sell me a new car immediately as a result of this activity it is highly likely that I will remember this promotion when I am looking to change my car.

So why don't you send your patients a birthday card every year? And when you send the card put an offer in it, lets say something like Happy Birthday from Sanderson Dental Practice, here's a voucher for £10.00 off the price of your next examination.

Just think how powerful that message is, it builds the bond between yourself and your patient and it is highly likely that they will use the voucher and attend the next examination.

With the possible exception of financial institutions and government agencies, how many other commercial organisations know their customers birthday? You will almost certainly be the only business that sends a birthday card.

I would even go to the length of handwriting a proper birthday card and then put a voucher in, to add that extra personal touch.

The big mistake that just about every business makes with direct mail or any other form of advertising is testing the effectiveness of different types of mailings. They send out thousands of a particular mail shot and wonder what went wrong when they receive a trickle of answers.

Now here's an interesting phrase "Statistical Predictability". In layman's terms this means that if you send out 1000 letters to your patients and receive 10 responses, it is highly likely that if you send out 2000 you'll receive around 20 responses.

So rather than spend an age coming up with what you think is the ideal direct mail shot, send out a few and see what happens, send out three versions of the same type of offer, maybe a different headline on each to around 250 recipients and see which one gets you the best return.

If one gets you five responses but another gets you ten, and the third gets you fifteen roll that one out. This is not rocket science but very few companies employ this testing because it takes a little time.

Now postcards are not the sexiest piece of marketing literature on the market, and you might think that nobody sends postcards any longer and you could well be right.

Well the fact that nobody else sends them out any longer is exactly the reason why you should be doing it!

If you can't bring yourself to take my advice about text messaging, postcards are probably the next best way to remind your patients about their upcoming appointment (OK neck and neck with an email).

But if you're going to spend all that time and effort producing a postcard to remind your patients about their upcoming appointment, why not use it to print some marketing information on it too.

It's the ideal medium to tell your patients about what you are doing at the moment, it might be a promotion on whitening, oral hygiene, or whatever message you want to send.

The good old postcard is almost a distant memory for most people so what do you think would happen if they receive one, (yes they read it). It's a bit like a text message although not quite as powerful, but most people do actually read postcards.

I would still be inclined to use text messaging as my primary way to communicate with my patients, if I were a practicing dentist but don't forget the old postcard.

So we've covered a whole host of ways to communicate with your patients/customers. You're probably wondering which you should use, well ideally use them all, if not use as many as you have the time to do.

In order to build loyalty with your patients, you need to communicate and communicate regularly, it is this that will enable you to have premium pricing and loyal patients.

Chapter Sixteen
Collaborative Marketing

This is an easy form of marketing, again very few business use it and that's another reason why you should. Collaborative Marketing is just about working hand in hand with another local none competing business.

For instance you could work with the local independent chemist, whereby every patient who visits you will receive a voucher to spend in the chemist and they would do the same for you. Or simply you put an advertisement for their business in your premises and they do the same for you.

It doesn't even have to be a company in the health business. You could work with the local florist, newsagent, restaurant, baker etc. Just look at the businesses in your high street and approach them to see if they would be interested in working with you.

If for instance you had an arrangement with the local florist, they might be prepared to give you a bouquet of flowers to display in your waiting room each week, with some sort of promotional message on the vase.

You could put the menus of the local restaurant in your waiting room, maybe with some photographs. This is really easy to do and costs very little.

Do you remember the promotion I highlighted in the last chapter with the BMW dealer and the restaurant working hand in hand, in this instance they're not even in the same town or county but they are close enough to work together. I suspect the owner of the car dealership eats in the restaurant or the owner of the restaurant buys his/her car at the BMW garage.

Chapter Seventeen
Top Ten Marketing Mistakes You Should Avoid

Before we go into the marketing mistakes let me share with you some really scary facts.

•Effective marketing is the ability of the business to consistently and repeatedly get people to buy the products or services they sell and extract as much profit out of each customer over the duration of the relationship.
•Marketing is critical to EVERY business.
•With no marketing or ineffective marketing, your prospects may never find out about the products or services you offer. These very services that they may need, want or that could benefit them and consequently, a sale may never be made.
•80% of small business will go out of business in the first five years.
•Of those that remain 80% will be gone in the next ten years.
•It takes more than low prices for a business to remain competitive in today's market.
•Marketing is THE major key to success in business.
•The major cause of business failure is not having enough customers buying from you on a regular and profitable basis.

So now I've scared the living daylights out of you let's have a look at the top ten marketing mistakes that particularly affect dentistry.

Marketing Mistake (1) Not having a Unique Selling Proposition (USP)

Your USP is what makes you different, why would a customer or patient come to you rather than someone else down the road? Your USP is what makes the difference between having a truly outstanding business or a faltering one.

As I write this book a major supermarket chain have committed to rolling out dental practices in its stores. This particular one is planning to roll out up to 200 sites over the next few years. Another one is opening three practices in their stores in Scotland, on a pilot scheme basis. If they come to your town how are you going to compete with them?

These new players are going to be centrally located, have a huge existing customer base, ample parking, loyalty schemes, in-store practice etc., with lots of marketing experience to fall back on. To compete with these guys you need to offer something different or outstanding. If not it is highly likely that you'll lose a proportion of your patients to them.

By using the techniques mentioned earlier in this book you can not only compete with these people, but beat them. But not only do you need to offer outstanding service, you need to communicate with your patients all the time. Make them feel like they are part of your practice, encourage that loyalty.

A great example of a fantastic USP (unique selling point) is Dominos Pizza. When they first started their company (strangely enough, making pizza) they struggled to make their mark.

They quickly realised that a large number of their customers were students who didn't cook and usually wanted to eat quickly. So they changed from being just another company that made Pizza to one that concentrated on delivering Pizza quicker than anyone else. Their slogan "Red Hot Pizza Delivered To Your Door In 30 Minutes Or Less Guaranteed" catapulted them into the big league of Pizza.

So let me give you a hint on how you can turn this dreaded CQC registration into a positive. If you have just installed a decontamination room/unit into your practice, write and tell all your patients. I'll guarantee you that your competitors haven't (even the Supermarkets). If you install instrument tracking software, tell your patients, put in your newsletter, email them, this is what makes you stand out and be different. So what is your USP?

Marketing Mistake (2) Failing to Use Testimonials

It never ceases to amaze me how many businesses don't use testimonials. Let's face it, if your friend, relative etc. recommends something to you, it is without doubt the best advertising that a company can get but most companies don't use it.

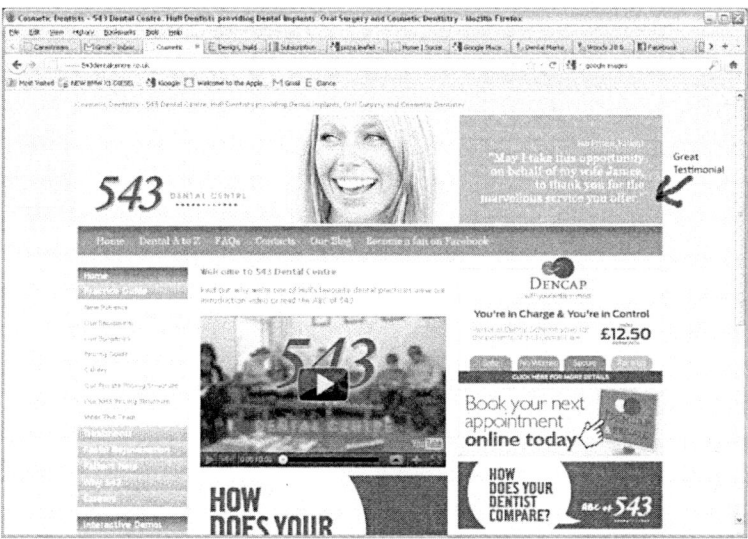

Great Testimonial right on the front page

I'm not sure how many of you use the Trip Advisor web site. Personally I will not book a hotel that doesn't have good testimonials on there. Just about all the more savvy web sites are now incorporating customer testimonials, such as Marks and Spencer and Amazon to list just two.

We are all sceptical of the marketing speak of companies, but will accept almost without question, the word of someone who is independent of that company even if we've never met them.

You should encourage your customers to give you testimonials, put them on your web site, in your Newsletters, in fact anywhere you can, even if it's a booklet of testimonials in your waiting room.

People don't like to be the first to do or try things especially if it involves parting with their money.

People don't buy for three main reasons (1) they can't afford it. (2) they have no need for it. (3) They don't trust the seller. There's not a lot you can do about reasons one and two, but three is the key. You have to develop the level of trust and believability that customers need to do business with you.

Getting testimonials is easy. Send a questionnaire, evaluation form, send a letter requesting a testimonial, ring them and ask. Use everything.

Marketing Mistake (3) Not keeping in touch with clients

In order to do battle with the likes of the mainstream supermarkets, you need to offer extraordinary service and that doesn't mean seeing your patients every six months or once a year.

You should be communicating with them at least once a month, use whatever means you can including Social Media, Email, Newsletters etc.

Just because a patient hasn't been to see you for a while, doesn't mean that they never want to see you every again. Your customers are no different than anyone else's. They all want to feel part of something and feel that they are important.

You might communicate with a customer or patient for several years and hear nothing at all back, but that doesn't mean that they don't want your services, it's because they don't want it just now.

I recently purchased a video camera. Now let me explain I am not the slightest bit interested in making home videos and have never been interested in video cameras.

But starting this business (Dental Marketing Expert), means that I have to communicate with my prospects and customers on a regular basis and one of the best ways is via video.

So buying a video camera suddenly became my number one priority and this is someone who has never been interested whatsoever. I had absolutely no idea what sort of video camera to buy, so I Googled "camcorder reviews" and studied the products for hours. After all that research I eventually bought one that a colleague recommended (do you see how this works).

So just because 90% of your customers don't want an implant today, tomorrow or next week doesn't mean that they won't want one next year. The same goes for whitening, root canal, orthodontics etc.

Marketing Mistake (4) Not using your 'Hidden Gold Mine'

A few facts for you to digest:

•It costs seven to eight times more to sell to a new customer/patient than to an existing one.
•Marketing costs can often exceed profits.
•It's far easier to do business with people that you already know.
•Many business actually lose money on each new customer they get.

Yes of course I'm talking about all the patients or customers you've seen over the years and are currently languishing in that practice management software you have.

The quickest way to grow profits is selling additional items to existing or dormant customers. At every opportunity up sell your services, or offer something different, such as oral education, whitening, hygienist etc.

You have what most business dream of and that's a patient/customer list sat right there on your premises. You know or you can find out exactly how often patients see you, when they last attended, what they buy or don't. This is the sort of information that supermarkets go to incredible lengths to find out, at great cost and you have it all because of the profession you're in.

You know their birthday, who their family is, maybe their wedding anniversary, if they smoke, their overall health etc. etc. This is a true gold mine and so few make use of it.

Marketing Mistake (5) Not Using Compelling Headlines
So if you still need new patients and customers after you've done all the above and you have to resort to advertising, say something that will grab their attention.

It's simply not good enough to just put your company name up there in bold type, which means absolutely nothing to your customers. If you want to see great examples of this open any page in the Yellow Pages and see advert after advert with a name as the main headline, it's a total waste of time and money.

On your web site say what you do on the front page (remember you have just eight seconds to keep their attention)! Having a pretty picture and your name on the landing page is a pointless exercise, unless you also have some sort of call to action as I showed earlier in the book.

The same goes for any other type of advertising press, magazine, mail shot etc. etc. its the headline that catches your attention.

Just think about when you read a newspaper. You scan the page but you're not looking at the stories, are you? What you are looking for are the headlines, to see if there's anything that catches your attention, and your advert is no different.

Newspapers have spent millions over the years perfecting this technique and television news is no different either. What's the first thing that happens when the news starts? That's right, they give you snippets of what they're going to be covering in the programme, they don't go straight into the first story, even if it's a massive one.

Marketing Mistake (6) Using Institutional Advertising

Do you want to build a brand, improve your name awareness or do you want to get more sales? It's a simple choice.

Most large companies go for the brand building model because they feel that the strength of the brand is all important and in many cases that is the right thing to do. The problem is that most of us are small businesses and brand really counts for nothing.

The likes of Coca Cola, Apple, Google, Microsoft for instance want it to be their products that you pick when you are in the market for a drink, computer, search engine or software etc. and when you get to be their size they are absolutely right in this approach.

Unfortunately this is the way that most small to medium sized companies also conduct their marketing. There is a corporate chain of dentists who spend a fortune on the image of their dental practices. All have to be branded properly following the company guide lines.

However given there is usually only one of their practices in a given city or town, what is the point? People tend to not go from town to town looking for a practice and almost certainly have no idea of the identity of a small chain of dental practices.

It is highly unlikely that you will ever have a business similar to Tesco, Sainsburys, Coca Cola etc. So do not fall into the trap of thinking you have to advertise and market like them.
You are looking to increase your revenues and profits and this type of advertising will never do it for you. Again I would suggest you look at your web site and ask yourself, would a patient come to us after spending eight seconds on this site?

Great image doesn't always guarantee great sales. Your strengths are not big brand, national or international coverage. Your strength is that you offer great service, you are on your customer's doorstep, you know your customers personally, you offer great service to a local community; shout that from the hill tops.

Marketing Mistake (7) Not Using The Internet
The internet is the most powerful way for you to communicate with you patients, customers, prospective patients etc. All the technologies are now coming together, TV, Computer, Mobile Device etc. into one big entertainment and communications centre.

How long do you imagine it's going to be before we don't have scheduled TV programs any longer? Everything will be on-demand, it pretty much is now. All TV's will in effect be large screen computers linked to the internet.

So if you're not using the internet now, start today. As I said earlier the days of Yellow Pages are pretty much gone already. Today, if anyone wants to find anything, the first place they look is the internet and if you're not on it they'll never find you.

And the internet isn't just about web sites either; it includes email, video, directories, speech (yes the podcast is very powerful too).

But simply putting up a web site won't answer your prayers, there are literally billions of web sites in the world, how do you think people are going to find you even if you have the most amazing web site on the planet?

And just finding you isn't the answer either, as I said earlier 99% of people visiting your web site will do nothing, the vast majority will spend less than eight seconds on your site!

You have to have a web strategy of (a) getting people there in the first place and (b) getting them to do something when they're there.

On-line appointment booking has been available for a few years now but barely any practices have bought into the concept. The arguments against is "We don't want patients accessing our appointment book", "It's too easy for them to cancel", "I might get a virus". Sorry but this just isn't true.

If you go online to book a theatre ticket, do you find the show you want to see and then pick up the phone to book, or do you book online. When you want to fly somewhere, do you go onto the web site, find the flight then call the airline?

No you can bet your life you don't, so why do you expect your patients to do the same, just think how much easier it would be if they could book and amend appointments online (remember <u>Unique Selling Point</u>).

We're talking about service here and if you get the odd bad apple that doesn't turn up for an appointment they booked online so be it, the other 95% of your patients will thank you for the choice.

The ability for you patients to book an appointment on-line should be on the front page of your web site, it is the reason for you having one isn't it?

I can think of nothing more important than patients being able to make appointments that they would not have normally made. Most of the rest of your web site is just telling them what you do and how well you might do it, who the team are etc. Just go onto a variety of dental web sites (not your own) and ask yourself "If I were looking for a dentist, what would make me want to book an appointment with this practice".

We all get spam email but we also receive email that we are not only happy to receive but miss it if it doesn't arrive in your in box and sometimes wonder where it is.

If you have a well thought out email strategy, this can be even more powerful than your web site. The key is making sure the recipients of your mail get something in return, don't just try and sell to them.

Marketing Mistake (8) Only Using A Small Number of Marketing Tools

"We're in the Yellow Pages and take out a few ads in the local press"

I can't tell you how often I've heard that one and people wonder why their advertising isn't working.

Even very large companies with large marketing budgets aren't that much better. They just spend a lot more money on pointless adverting doing the same thing over and over again, without the slightest clue how well its actually doing.

If you're going to do marketing, do lots of it and try everything. But don't go full on and book a year's worth of ads in the local press, test, test and test again.

If something doesn't work, try something different, change the wording, the offer etc. Don't just have a web site and expect everyone to flock to you, they won't. Your marketing campaign needs to be coordinated and tested. Visit my web site www.dentalmarketingexpert.co.uk and book a consultation - I can help (sorry for the plug).

Marketing Mistake (9) Not charging the "Perfect Price" for your product or service

Here's how just about every business arrives at its pricing.

- You look at what your competitors charge.
- You decide 'where' you want your customers to view you – are you low priced, middle of the road or high end.
- You then price your product or service based on the results of these two scenarios.

The truth is that if you provide excellent value – people will flock to your business and pay you handsomely for the privilege.

Often people make the mistake of thinking that price is the main issue in the mind of their clients. Nothing could be further from the truth. If that were the case we'd all be driving the cheapest cars, wearing the cheapest clothes, shoes, eating the cheapest food etc. etc.

But that doesn't mean that you can just increase your prices tomorrow, quite the opposite. People buy on their perceived value of the product or service you offer. I'm not particularly into cars and find it difficult to get excited about them; however I still drive a BMW. People ask what I think of it, and by and large, I say I like it. Now we all know that BMW's are not the cheapest car on the market, equally they're not the most expensive. I bought it because I valued it highly enough to pay maybe five times the price of the cheapest car on the market, which would have done the job for me just as well.

I've mentioned this several times during this book. It's all about increasing your perceived value to your customers, so that they will want to stay with you whatever happens and when you increase your prices they will happily pay rather than move.

Sometimes customers move from one supplier to another because they simply want a change (this happens quite often with cars). Other times they really fall out with the supplier over what they perceive to be poor service or shoddy goods. But most of us change because we didn't think the service we were getting was worth what we paid for it.

Lots of times you'll ask a customer or ex-patient why they left and they'll tell you your prices were too high. What they really mean is that they weren't <u>getting value for money</u>.

All the previous pages of this book have been aimed at one thing and that is to improve the perceived value of the service you offer. We may call it marketing but really it's about getting the message to your customers that you offer incredible service. Your products and services are extra special and you will always go the extra yard for your customers. If you can reach this plateau you really have reached the marketing nirvana.

I have had many conversations with dentists during these economically difficult times and often they tell me "it's getting harder to fill the appointment book and patients aren't coming as often as they used to". When I've asked what he/she has done about it they say "I've increased my prices".

As I said earlier, there is absolutely no problem increasing your prices but it has to be when you are offering exceptional value to your customers, if not they'll simply drift away.

Marketing Mistake (10) Not Having a Referral Process or System
Without a shadow of a doubt referral business is the best type of business you can have. You rarely have to compete on price and these customers tend to be people you enjoy working with. Better still, you'll find that you convert a much higher percentage of referrals into clients or customers.

If you get a referral from 50% of your patients every year what sort of difference would that make to your business? Massive.

However getting referrals is very much dependent on the previous chapter. If your patients think that you give outstanding value for money and do a terrific job, they will, without doubt, refer you without hesitation. On the other hand if you are not giving extra-ordinary service, the opposite will happen.

Getting a referral is very easy, first of all simply ask if a patient would refer you to a friend. or ask them if they know anyone who you could send a letter or text, email to etc.

You could set up a system whereby if a patient refers someone to your practice, you give them a discount on some treatment, it's up to you how you do it but start some sort of system today.

Extra Mistake (this needs to be included)
Failing to Calculate The Cost Of Losing a Patient/Customer
When you lose a patient/customer you may think as most other business do. Hey ho, never mind, we've just lost 'x' pounds (however much you charge them per year etc.) Unfortunately the real cost is much more.

The cost of losing a customer

1.You lose the unhappy customer		1
2.He/she tells ten other friends/family		10
3.They in turn tell six other people	60	
4.Total bad experience shared with others	71	
5.At least 25% won't come to you because of this	18	
6.Average lifetime value of customer	£2,000	
7.Lost income over 10 years	£37,000	

OK, so we just made up these figures as an example, but you need to be aware of just how powerful an unhappy customer can be, in fact more powerful than a happy customer who gives you a glowing reference.

Going the extra mile, giving extra-ordinary service is crucial to a thriving business.

Chapter 18
It's all down to you

We've covered a lot of ground over the last few pages. If you act on every one of my hint, I guarantee that your practice or business will not only survive but it will thrive.

Unfortunately it is my experience that most of you will do nothing. A few will try a couple of these hints and then give up. Maybe 5% will really give it a try and they will succeed.

The big problem for most small to medium sized businesses is that they are too busy running the business to think about marketing. But marketing is the business, without it there would be no business.

It's not a myth that when times get tough most business slash the marketing budget, but that's exactly the wrong thing to do. You need to integrate a marketing plan into your core business, as without it you can never grow.

If you can't do it yourself you should call in a professional such as myself to help, but you need to do something or you'll fail.
A great phrase I use all the time is "how do you know when you'll get there if you don't know where you're going", this is so true and without goals you literally are at sea.

Marketing your practice/business should be an integral part of those goals, so if for instance if your goal is to become the best dental practice in your area (great goal incidentally), how are you going to measure that?

If you don't take patient surveys, have referral systems in place, use testimonials, how will you know that you are in fact the "best practice in the area".

An easier one is a financial goal. If, for instance, your goal is to double your profits in three years? In order to do this you need to sit down and plan (a) is this achievable (b) how are you going to do it? In theory you could just double your prices and you may be one of the very lucky people that get away with it, but most of us aren't that lucky and need to have a plan in order to achieve the goal.

Your goal may be "I want to be the best employer" . Once again very honourable, but if your business is struggling to make ends meet, it is unlikely you'll have the time or inclination to meet this objective.

So you see marketing is integral to just about any goal you set yourself and doing it well is not always easy, but when done well, the rewards are amazing.

The very best marketers, indeed the best business people, make lots of mistakes. We all know about the successes of Richard Branson and Virgin, but he launches many new companies and ideas, the majority of which fail, but that doesn't mean he fails.

He just takes more risks than the rest of us and that is the same for all successful business people, as they are prepared to go that extra mile, do that something that is just a bit different and be prepared to fail, but when they do, they just get on with it and try something different.

So just because you try a mail shot or email campaign or radio advertisement and it doesn't seem to work, that doesn't mean you should give up, try different wording, use different graphics, try another publication and you will reap the rewards eventually.

There are many businesses that try the odd thing and fail but then give up at that point, inevitably they are the businesses that stay in the doldrums and never really see success.

The only person who can make all this happen is you, as the owner or managing director of the business. You have to have an achievable business plan and you have to have a web site that is integral to the business and that works (most companies don't).

There's an old saying that goes "if at first you don't succeed try and try again". Whilst that's partially correct just don't keep trying the same thing that fails over and over again.

The right marketing will ensure the survival and growth of your company, I hope that I've given you enough ideas to find the one's that work for you.

The Author Neil Sanderson

FALSE IDOLS

Karla Marie Sweet is a British-American actor, screenwriter, novelist and dramaturg born and based in Manchester, UK. Recent acting credits include acclaimed road movie *Black Dog* and season 2 of Hulu's *No Man's Land*. As a writer, she has multiple television credits to her name and her comedy-drama script *DaSilva & Sharp* landed her on the 2023 Brit List. Her theatre credits include *Cheetham Hill* (for the Royal Exchange), This Little Relic (BBC Radio 3 and the Belgrade Theatre) and *Othello* (Watermill Theatre). Her speculative fiction novel *Another Life* was released as an Audible Original in September 2024. *False Idols* is Karla's print debut.